HARDY'S
WESSEX

HARDY'S WESSEX

Desmond Hawkins
with photographs by Anthony Kersting

MACMILLAN LONDON

For Marita
  and Pauline
    and Robert
who should have had a volume apiece —
had I but world enough and time

Designed by Robert Updegraff

ISBN 0 333 34115 5

First published 1983 by
Macmillan London Limited
London and Basingstoke

Associated companies in Auckland, Dallas,
Delhi, Dublin, Hong Kong, Johannesburg,
Lagos, Manzini, Melbourne, Nairobi,
New York, Singapore, Tokyo, Washington
and Zaria

Filmset in Apollo by Filmtype Services Limited,
Scarborough, North Yorkshire.

Contents

CHAPTER ONE

The Origin of Wessex

In his old age Thomas Hardy entered in one of his notebooks a thought which plainly reflected his own experience – 'I am convinced that it is better for a writer to know a little bit of the world remarkably well than to know a great part of the world remarkably little'. The dry sententious manner and the balanced symmetry of the construction do not conceal the inner personal strength of his ties with the West Country, where he was born and spent the greater part of his life. *Wessex* as we know it today is his creation. It is the little bit of the world that he knew remarkably well. Something of Hardy's own self speaks in the voice of Grace Melbury in *The Woodlanders* when she says, 'I love dear old Hintock, *and the people in it*, fifty times better than all the Continent!'

Nonetheless Hardy well understood the limitations of provincial life. In his first published novel, *Desperate Remedies*, he commented, 'Provincial towns trying to be lively are the dullest of dull things'. He himself might in the end be described as a regional man but not a provincial one. He prided himself on being as much at ease in London as in Dorchester. Indeed the love-hate relationship between Wessex and the metropolis was a factor of constant relevance and intensity in Hardy's creative life. He was of that first generation of ambitious young men to whom the railway offered an escape from the rural obscurity of Dorset to the stimulation, the wide intellectual horizon, of the capital city. The two contrasting modes of feeling – for his native soil and for his cultural Mecca – entwine, sometimes fusing, sometimes pulling asunder, always with varying degrees of emphasis and never finally resolved. In the complexity of his genius this tension is a primary factor.

An early poem, 'From Her in the Country', expresses it clearly. The speaker has tried to suppress thoughts of the 'crass clanging town' and cling to the belief that rural scenes are worth more 'than all man's urban shows'. But she admits she failed in this highminded aim

> And mused again on city din and sin,
> Longing to madness I might move therein!

The date that Hardy added to the poem is significant – 1866, when he was living in London at lodgings in Westbourne Park Villas. Writing later of this period of his life Hardy recalled that, before he was thirty, he had had 'between five and six years' constant and varied experience' of London. He took a pride in claiming that he knew 'every street and alley west of St. Paul's like a born Londoner, which he was often supposed to be'.

In his middle years he liked to move to London each year for the fashionable period of the Season and he was no stranger to the Athenaeum and the Savile Club. When he returned to Dorchester and completed the building of Max Gate in 1885 he was sometimes lonely in this new permanent home in Wessex and wanted to get away from it. To John Addington Symonds, who was then living in Switzerland, Hardy in 1889 confided: 'I, too, am in a sense exiled. I was obliged to leave Town after a severe illness some years ago – and the spot on which I live here is very lonely.' Similarly to Edmund Gosse in 1886, Hardy wrote, 'Our life here is lonely and cottage-like'. To Gosse again the following year, after a springtime visit to Italy and a summer in London, Hardy wrote from Max Gate, 'I am quite frantic to go off somewhere again – but must not'.

If there were times, then, when he felt himself imprisoned in Wessex, there were also and increasingly those countervailing occasions when he rejoiced at the thought that

> citizens dream of the south and west,
> And so do I.

His personal discovery of Wessex was a gradual and intermittent process. In the early stages of his literary career he evidently saw himself as a satirist, operating from an independent 'bohemian' standpoint. His more pointed and severe shafts were to be directed at high society, while a kinder teasing style would satirise the

Max Gate,
Dorchester

'quaintness' of village life in Wessex. Hardy frequently used the word 'quaint' in this way, reckoning that it was the comic and ingenuous qualities of his native background that would be most acceptable to the larger and more sophisticated audience to which he was addressing himself. From *Under the Greenwood Tree* to *Tess of the d'Urbervilles* is a long march and a hard-won advance. The village names of Tantrum Clangley and Puddle-sub-Mixen are supportable in the Wessex of Hardy's early novels but unthinkable in his later ones.

He coined the word *Wessex* in its modern sense – or revived and adapted it – in *Far from the Madding Crowd*, as he explained in a subsequent preface:

> It was in the chapters of *Far from the Madding Crowd*, as they appeared month by month in a popular magazine, that I first ventured to adopt the word 'Wessex' from the pages of early English history, and give it a fictitious significance as the existing name of the district once included in that extinct kingdom. The series of novels I projected being mainly of the kind called local, they seemed to require a territorial definition of some sort to lend unity to their scene. Finding that the area of a single county did not afford a canvas large enough for this purpose, and that there were objections to an invented name, I disinterred the old one.
>
> Since then the appellation which I had thought to reserve to the horizons and landscapes of a partly real, partly dream-country, has become more and more popular as a practical provincial definition; and the dream-country has, by degrees, solidified into a utilitarian region which people can go to, take a house in, and write to the papers from.

In that moment of decision the word *Wessex*, as we now use it, was born. Two consequences followed from it. The first, the easier and the most obvious was the disappearance from Hardy's writings of the names of counties. As he noted in *The Life*:

> So far did he carry this idea of the unity of Wessex that he used to say he had grown to forget the crossing of county boundaries within the ancient kingdom – in this respect being quite unlike the poet Barnes, who was 'Dorset' emphatically.

The other consequence was the replacement of the names of towns, villages and individual buildings with fictitious ones of his own invention. There were distinguished precedents to follow. When he gave Reading the name of Aldbrickham he was displacing the earlier pseudonym 'Belford Regis' bestowed on the town by Mary Russell Mitford; and if Salisbury is insecure in its claim to be Barchester it can find comfort in its identity as Hardy's Melchester. The coining of spurious place-names was a feature of the nineteenth-century novel. Hardy did not initiate the practice though he carried it further, in a fuller and more systematic way, than any of his predecessors.

There were uncertainties at first in his method and some anomalies remained to the end. The very next thing he wrote after *Far from the Madding Crowd* was the short story 'Destiny and a Blue

Marshwood Vale, seen from Pilsdon Pen

5

Ashmore pond in Cranborne Chase

Cloak'; here the characters live in the village of Netherbury, which Hardy renamed Cloton, but the places they visit are given their actual names – Beaminster, Maiden Newton, Weymouth. The conversion of names to fit conformably within the Wessex convention was a gradual process, with Hardy finding fresh opportunities to revise and add to his personal gazetteer when the proofs of a new edition of one novel or another came to him for approval.

Even so an occasional ambiguity remains unresolved. Where, one may ask, is the true and uncontestable Trantridge? The Trantridge of *Tess of the d'Urbervilles* is always understood to be in reality Pentridge, which lies at the end of a by-road running south-east from the main Salisbury-Blandford road. Hardy clearly intended this identification, but Frank Pinion has drawn attention to the Trantridge mentioned in the group of tales collectively entitled *A Few Crusted Characters*. As this other Trantridge is described it lies *on* the same Salisbury-Blandford road, not in a turning off it, and it is so near to Blandford that it can only be Pimperne or Tarrant Hinton. When the story first appeared, in a periodical, the place was called Tranton, subsequently changed to Trantridge. Denys Kay-Robinson's suggestion that 'Tranton' is a characteristically Hardyesque fictional version of Tarrant Hinton seems to put the issue beyond doubt. Whether by design or neglect, Hardy gave the name of Trantridge to two villages which lie about ten miles from each other.

Setting aside a rare lapse of that sort, the general development of the nomenclature of Wessex observed the principle of retaining the actual names of natural features, such as hills and rivers, and concentrating the author's inventiveness on human habitations. Often the fictitious name is a transparent variation on the original. There were circumstances, more particularly in his earlier works, when Hardy wished to prevent a too close identification – as for example in *A Pair of Blue Eyes*, which drew on the scenes of his courtship of his first wife, Emma, and might have embarrassed her relatives – but in the main it was not as a device for secrecy that Wessex was of value to Hardy. It had more precise and practical values for a professional novelist.

In the first place its fictional nature gave elasticity to the constraints of literal topography. 'Casterbridge' could accommodate any amount of poetic licence which Dorchester would have been compelled to deny. It is a part of the novelist's art to fuse together attributes drawn from several sources, to expand or contract distances at will, to blend accurate observation with the play of a free imagination. Not without reason did Hardy take care to emphasise that his Wessex was a 'partly real, partly dream-country'. No matter how convincingly we may translate some item of his fiction into fact, it must remain at best an approximation.

There was another advantage for him as a novelist in this concept of Wessex. It gave a continuity and a momentum to his books. The unity it provided even amounted to an additional sort of copyright. Other writers might address themselves to Salisbury or Weymouth but they could scarcely hope to enter Melchester or Budmouth. Hardy's consciousness of this benefit is evident in a letter he wrote to one of his publishers:

> Could you, whenever advertising my books, use the words 'Wessex novels' at the head of the list? I mean, instead of 'By

7

T.H.', 'T.H.'s Wessex Novels' or something of the sort? I find that the name *Wessex*, wh. I was the first to use in fiction, is getting to be taken up everywhere: and it would be a pity for us to lose the right to it for want of asserting it.

Although Hardy chose *Wessex Poems* as the title for his first collection of poems he made no attempt as a poet to achieve the conformity of place-names that he judged to be necessary in his novels and short stories. 'Mellstock' and Stinsford both appear in his *Collected Poems*. The actual Hermitage and the fictitious 'Ivel' even occur together in the same line. To replace a real name with an already established fictional one is easy enough in prose but often virtually impossible in verse. Hardy evidently used real names at the time of composition in some instances, and decided to retain them; in other cases he had a preference at the outset for one of his invented names. For the poet, as distinct from the novelist, there was no hard-and-fast rule. For the reader it may indeed be a part of the fascination of Hardy's poetry that it evokes a sense of place in which dream and reality become increasingly hard to separate.

There is one further point to be made about Hardy's Wessex. So far from being an isolated innovation in our literature it is clearly a part of the nineteenth century's absorption in the subjects of regional identity, dialect, survivals of folk-lore and legend, and anything that could be recognised as a local flavour in landscape or people. Previously it had been the purpose of writers from the Restoration to the Regency to establish national norms of language, of social behaviour, of aesthetic taste; eventually to define and entrench the genteel society of Georgian England – and more precisely of Georgian London and south-eastern England. Life outside that pale was ignored or represented only in jocular buffooneries: it was no fit subject for a serious mind to contemplate.

What disturbed this Augustan composure was a curiosity about the 'Gothick' past. The poet William Shenstone's taste for artificially 'ruinated' priories and the publication in 1765 of Bishop Percy's *Reliques of Ancient English Poetry* pointed the way to Coleridge, Wordsworth, Scott and the incoming tide of the great Romantic movement which was to dominate the nineteenth century with its emotional excesses, its cultivation of morbidity and horror, its

A cottage and blossom at Ashmore

antiquarian pursuits and its intellectual radicalism. Under the pressure of new ideas the venerable deities of classical mythology had to yield space to accommodate Arthur and Guinevere, Tristan and Isolde and many another whose feet had never touched the soil of Greece or Rome. At several levels the Victorians undertook what might be described as a national stock-taking, turning out neglected mediaeval cupboards and confronting familiar landscapes with a new set of questions.

Where the eighteenth-century traveller seemed to find little interest in rural scenes except the 'seats' of the nobility and gentry, which came into view and were assiduously catalogued in contemporary road-guides, his Victorian counterpart was increasingly interested in the tokens of prehistory – the grave-mounds and occasional monuments of stone with which local legends and superstitions tended to be linked. What the Age of Reason had been apt to dismiss was now seized upon by the Romantic imagination. The

*'Haggard Egdon':
a tumulus on
Rainbarrow Hill,
Duddle Heath*

forms of natural history, from the stones of geology to the flight of birds, similarly aroused a new enthusiasm. Imperceptibly the living past and the picturesque present coalesced to create a spirit of place, a *genius loci*, which we can now recognise as a special attribute of nineteenth-century literature.

We should be hard put to identify the Fielding country or the Milton country on any map of Britain, but there is no doubt in any literate mind as to where to look for the Lakeland of the Poets or the Brontë country or the Lorna Doone country – or Hardy's Wessex. Certain types of landscape, certain forms of speech, will at once evoke for us a particular part of the country and the work of a particular writer. This close concern with the historical and physical context and the human characteristics of a region is a striking feature in the literature of the last century and the early decades of the present one.

Since then the general mobility of our contemporaries, added to the radical transformation of rural life, has disintegrated and dispersed the old cultural unity in which Hardy found his inspiration. The regional flowering of the West Country began with Barnes's poetry and the founding of 'Wessex' in *Far from the Madding Crowd*. It gained strength and variety from the writings of Richard Jefferies and R. D. Blackmore, the archaeology of Pitt-Rivers, the folk-song collections of Cecil Sharp and Ralph Vaughan Williams, the adopted literary talents of W. H. Hudson and Edward Thomas, and the astonishing theatrical success between the wars of Eden Philpotts's Devonshire plays, *The Farmer's Wife* and *Yellow Sands*. During the span of Hardy's lifetime there grew up in England almost a cult of the romantic West Country, finding a glamour in its style of speech, its scenery and its rural way of life – a cult which has been displaced in the past thirty years by the more insistent and clamorous tones of the northern cities.

To set Hardy's Wessex within this larger cultural context is not to diminish his personal achievement but to enhance it. It is the mark of a great writer that he should respond to the deepest forces within an epoch and that his work should help to define that epoch. The Wessex that Hardy bequeathed to us – in part real, in part dream – has the timelessness and universality that belong to a work of art, but also a vividly detailed particularity of time and place. To explore Wessex in those terms is the purpose of this book.

11

CHAPTER TWO

Mellstock

The traditional way of defining the territory of a parish or some other unit of land – for example, a chase – was to beat the bounds, to make a perambulation of the perimeter and record enduring landmarks. In later years the recollections of those who had taken part in such a perambulation were of great importance whenever there was a dispute. To make a lasting impression on the minds of youthful participants there was allegedly a practice in some cases of administering a literal beating on the spot, though perhaps it was only a token ritual, if not quite apocryphal. Of the first beating of the bounds of Wessex there can be only one witness, and unexpectedly he proves to be less reliable than one might have assumed. His testimony is given in writing in *The Life of Thomas Hardy* by Florence Emily Hardy thus:

> A peculiarity in the local descriptions running through all Hardy's writings may be instanced here – that he never uses the word 'Dorset', never names the county at all (except possibly in an explanatory footnote), but obliterates the names of the six counties, whose area he traverses in his scenes, under the general appellation of 'Wessex'.

Six counties? The central core provides three: Dorset, Wiltshire and Somerset. Cornwall must be included, and with it therefore the intervening Devon. That leaves only one place to fill, but two candidates – Hampshire and Berkshire. 'Avon' incidentally is irrelevant here, since it did not exist in Hardy's lifetime, but there were always seven counties providing the settings for his novels and short stories. His reference to 'six' is particularly interesting therefore because it appears to indicate something more than a momentary aberration, as we can see in examining the 'official' map of Wessex in its final form. Here Cornwall is given the name *Off Wessex*, implying that Hardy recognised its historical independence as a separate kingdom which would have been an alien constituent of the Saxon realm. To an imaginative mind Tristan and King Alfred must seem uneasy bedfellows.

In the full formulation of the Wessex map Hardy named Somerset *Outer Wessex*, Devon *Lower Wessex* and Hampshire *Upper Wessex* – the distinctions of Lower and Upper suggesting a relationship to London. I am reminded of a Devonshire lady who described me as belonging in this sense to 'people from up the line' – having in her thoughts the railway line from Plymouth. Of the remainder, *North Wessex* was Hardy's equivalent to Berkshire but with the city of Oxford brought across the county boundary. Wiltshire and Dorset are *Mid* and *South Wessex* respectively.

For the majority of Hardy's readers Wessex will remain a dream-country that they will never visit outside the covers of his books. Others will make a pilgrimage to satisfy their curiosity about Caster-bridge and Bulbarrow and Egdon Heath; and by no means are these pilgrims British only. In any summer, and particularly during one of the Hardy Festivals, you will find Americans, Japanese, Europeans taking snapshots of the birthplace at Higher Bockhamp-ton, visiting the Hardy family graves in Stinsford churchyard, wandering through Dorchester or Weymouth, going on conducted tours of some especially evocative and relevant parts of 'the Hardy country'. What they seek, and what they most value, can vary greatly from one individual to the next. Two examples that come to mind are the Japanese lady, a university lecturer, who wanted to see heather and gorse, and take specimens back to Tokyo to show her students; and the Canadian whose life had been spent in the open prairie country of Canada and who found the compact intimacy of the Dorset countryside such a 'revelation', to use his own word, that it changed his whole conception of the novels.

To satisfy these various requirements for information about Wessex there is already a specialist literature. In particular the decoding of Hardy's fictional names has become a scholarly pursuit in its own right: details of the principal books in this category are given in the select bibliography (page 198). The excellent pamphlets

13

of the Thomas Hardy Society should also be mentioned here as particularly suitable for those who want to explore a district associated with one particular novel.

It is not my intention to add to that literature, and certainly not to duplicate it by doing over again what has already been done adequately and well. For some a straightforward literary pilgrimage can add substance and vividness to one's appreciation. On the other hand it can disenchant because, with the passing of time, so much has changed; the pristine quality has deteriorated or faded or vanished completely. I confess to an uneasy suspicion that the Tintern Abbey I sometimes visit is not the Tintern Abbey that inspired Wordsworth, that Hardy's Egdon Heath is not the heath of the Bovington tank training-ground or the Winfrith Atomic Research Station. I take comfort from the thought that Hardy shared this same uneasiness when he wrote his 'Meditations on a Holiday'. This poem has the subtitle 'A new theme to an old folk-measure' and is dated May 1921, so it is a sprightly bit of teasing by an octogenarian. The first verse poses a familiar question:

> 'Tis a May morning,
> All-adorning,
> No cloud warning
> > Of rain today.
> Where shall I go to,
> Go to, go to? –
> Can I say No to
> > Lyonnesse-way?

He decides he *can* say No because what he would want to rediscover is no longer there. The glory has departed. He next considers Stratford-on-Avon and Lakeland, with the same result. He contemplates a pilgrimage to the haunts of Scott, of Burns, of Shelley, only to realise that their spirits have fled from their once familiar scenes. The visible remains are no more than husks devoid of life. In the closing verses he imagines the poets looking down with pitying amusement at his vain attempt to recall them to the shrines that literary pilgrims visit:

> If, on lawns Elysian,
> With a broadened vision
> And a faint derision

Conscious be they,
How they might reprove me
That these fancies move me,
Think they ill behoove me,
    Smile, and say:

'What! – our hoar old houses,
Where the bygone drowses,
Nor a child nor spouse is
    Of our name at all?
Such abodes to care for,
Inquire about and bear for,
And suffer wear and tear for –
    How weak of you and small!'

*Hardy's birthplace
at Higher
Bockhampton*

My aim is therefore a different sort of exploration of the Wessex scene – more of a personal celebration of a part of my native country that I have come to know with a knowledge and a love that converge from three different sources. There is first of all the Wessex I can see today – a countryside, beautiful in its own right, but with the added attraction that many of its associations with Hardy are still relatively unchanged, easy to identify and full of interest for those who come endowed already with some familiarity with his books. Then there is the Wessex that Hardy himself knew and which retains its original freshness in his pages. Lastly there is all that body of history and related literature which extends and amplifies our appreciation of the West Country, and from which in many instances Hardy himself drew some of his material.

Blended together these three sources present a Wessex which has an organic nature, unfolding and developing, living and dying, in a perspective which stretches back from today to the ancestral world from which Hardy emerged. To bemoan nostalgically the changes wrought in the course of a hundred and fifty years, or to avert one's eyes from them, is pointless. Much that we might like to see when we visit Wessex is gone for ever: I have no wish to pretend otherwise and to fudge the issue by searching desperately for *olde worlde* survivals.

Accordingly what I shall be seeking throughout this book is the interplay between the past and the present, the way in which a landscape and a culture gradually acquire their unique and abiding flavour: not something frozen rigid. Perhaps I can usefully borrow a musical metaphor here and speak of a harmony in which the bass will be Hardy's voice, a continuing strand of quotations from his writings; while the treble will embody the modern Wessex as I have learnt to appreciate it over the past thirty years.

Considered as it is presented in Hardy's map, Wessex may seem rather more unwieldy and extensive than the 'little bit of the world' that a writer might know 'remarkably well', even granting that he lived to be eighty-eight and was an indefatigable cyclist in his prime. From Oxford to Penzance is a long way. Moreover Land's End itself is not quite our journey's end, for the story 'A Mere Interlude' beckons us on to the Isles of Lyonesse, *alias* The Scillies, just as *The Mayor of Casterbridge* and *The Well-Beloved* make a case for taking in the Channel Islands during our travels. It is no disrespect to Hardy to say that his interest in some parts of Wessex is more perfunctory than in others. North Wessex, for example, is difficult to recognise as authentic Hardy country. The plot of *Jude the Obscure* exposes the fact that the rest of Wessex in 1890 had no university; and the annexation of Oxford as the 'Christminster' of the story was therefore a necessity. For the Judes of modern Wessex the universities of Bristol, Southampton and Exeter are more accessible, in both senses of the word.

The sprinkling of names over the Wessex map with a degree of evenhandedness may easily conceal the striking variations in the intensity of Hardy's interest in a locality. It is in the end the dream worlds of the Vale of the Little Dairies, of Egdon Heath, of Wessex Heights, that draw us to explore this haunted and haunting countryside where his name seems to be written everywhere and yet invisible.

I therefore take as the principal themes for my exploration those areas of Wessex which most dynamically vitalised Hardy's imagination; and the first must be the home-parish of the Hardys, Stinsford ('Mellstock') and more particularly the hamlet of Higher Bockhampton where Hardy was born in 1840 in the cottage his great-grandfather, John Hardy, had built in 1801 for his newly married son Thomas – the first of three generations of Thomases to live there. The cottage is now owned by the National Trust and is open to the public at reasonable times or by appointment.

The original Ordnance Survey map of 1811 shows the hamlet as New Bockhampton. Bockhampton proper was what is now known as Lower Bockhampton. In *The Life* Hardy claims that the family home was the first to be built in the vicinity. In the poem 'Domicilium' he recalls his grandmother's account of the place when she first settled there: it was overgrown with brambles, furze and thorn, which only later gave way to gardens and orchards as other homesteads were built. What is most vivid in her memory is the loneliness and wildness of the place:

> 'Our house stood quite alone, and those tall firs
> And beeches were not planted. Snakes and efts
> Swarmed in the summer days, and nightly bats
> Would fly about our bedrooms. Heathcroppers
> Lived on the hills, and were our only friends;
> So wild it was when first we settled here.'

17

That poem, according to Hardy, was the earliest of his to survive: written at about the time of his grandmother's death in 1857 or within the next two or three years. Much later, in 1902, he enshrined her in one of his best poems, with the simple title 'One We Knew'. It is a powerful evocation of his childhood, when he and the other Hardy children sat by the fireside listening to the old woman's tales of maypole and country dance, of the French Revolution and the rise of Bonaparte, of creaking gibbets and the screams of children whipped at the cart's tail. Looking back over half a century he conjures up the image of the compelling teller of tales:

With cap-framed face and long gaze into the embers –
    We seated round her knees –
She would dwell on such dead themes, not as one who remembers,
    But rather as one who sees.

Hers was the prophetic quality which impressed so deeply on Hardy his abiding sense of a long continuity extending into the distant past. In no other writer is there a more tenacious rootedness in folk-memory. In his voice one seems to hear the accents not of one generation but of many.

Although the A35 trunk-road is no distance away, the Hardy cottage at Higher Bockhampton preserves the atmosphere of 'a lonely and silent spot between woodland and heathland', as it was when Hardy was born there. The building itself has undergone some alterations, as might be expected in the course of nearly two hundred years. The chimney-corner, wide and brilliantly white as Hardy recalled it, where he had sat and listened to his elders 'by the embers in hearthside ease', was replaced during his lifetime.

The legend of the oxen kneeling at midnight on Christmas Eve was one of the hearthside tales that found expression long afterwards in Hardy's poetry. Another of the grandmother's visions, of an ancient Merrie England with beribboned maypoles and wild dancing, as 'breeched and kerchiefed partners whirled', was reinforced by the active tradition among the Hardys of fiddle-playing at country dances. At the age of four Hardy was given a toy accordion; as a boy he learned to tune a violin and accompany his father in playing at local dances. Often he danced at home to the jigs and hornpipes and other country dances that his father played in the evenings. It is pleasant to imagine the cottage as the scene sometimes

*'So wild it was':
the Hardy
homestead seen
from Thorncombe
Wood*

The river Frome at Lower Bockhampton

of such local dances as the Dorset Broom Dance, in which something akin to a sword-dance is performed with broom handles lying cross-wise on the floor instead of swords.

Hardy's love of dancing and the music that accompanied it was born in the cottage and remained a strong factor in his own personality and in his writings. When he went to live in London as a young man he visited, as a devout pilgrim might visit a shrine, the famous dancing-places which for him had been just glamorous names: 'Reminiscences of a Dancing Man' recaptures 'the deep

Drum-polka's booms' and all the excitement associated with Almack's, gay Cremorne and The Argyle. In *The Return of the Native* Hardy described Eustacia's recognition of dancing as 'that most subtle of lures' and commented:

> To dance with a man is to concentrate a twelvemonth's regulation fire upon him in the fragment of an hour. To pass to courtship without acquaintance, to pass to marriage without courtship, is a skipping of terms reserved for those alone who tread this royal road.

The short stories 'The History of the Hardcombes' and 'The Fiddler of the Reels' are grounded in the emotional powers that dancing releases, as is that superb narrative poem 'The Dance at the Phoenix'. In barndance or ballroom or open air gipsying the haunting music that he learned in the family circle runs like a thread through Hardy's entire life. In one of his last poems, written when he was eighty-six and had just heard of the death of Agnes Grove, his mind turned at once to the final occasion when he had danced out-of-doors. She had been his partner at the Larmer Tree Gardens thirty years earlier: now it was too late to cherish the hope he had so often felt 'to dance with that fair woman yet once more'.

If the birthplace could retain some bygone echo of the music once played within its walls, it would not be dance music only. No reader of *Under the Greenwood Tree* needs to be reminded that the elder Hardys were the mainstay of the church musicians. Hardy's knowledge of hymns, carols, anthems and psalms began in the cradle, continued at Stinsford church and Sunday school, and combined with his Bible-reading to give him his remarkably close familiarity with Christian thought and feeling. One of his childhood games was to pretend he was conducting a church service, with his grandmother as the congregation.

Music, sacred and profane, was the bright element in his heritage. There were darker tones also, in the talk of the elders. The fear of an invasion of the Dorset coast by the French had been no less real to them than the fear in 1940 of an invasion by the Germans. The original Ordnance Survey map of Dorset, referred to earlier, had been prepared not for civil but for military reasons. The beacons along the hills of Dorset had a severely practical purpose as warning signals if an enemy landed in force.

21

Still darker in tone were the glimpses of savagery and violence beneath the outward serenity of Wessex life. From his grandmother the boy learned to expect what he later saw – a public hanging. Her recollection of the whipping of children as a 'cure' for vagrancy is well founded in fact. An entry in Cranborne parish register, for example, records as a routine event that Edward Bayly, aged about 10, and Mary Bayly, aged about 12, were whipped as vagrants and sent towards their last place of residence in Sussex. Both were described as having 'a pale thin visage', which hardly seems surprising in the circumstances.

Life within the family circle of the Hardys was prosperous enough but the surrounding atmosphere of repression and desperation among the less fortunate must have been felt. The agricultural riots which swept through southern England in 1830 brought violence to Puddletown, with the burning of ricks and smashing of machinery. In 1833 some labourers at Tolpuddle attempted to form what would have been, in effect, the first trade-union – with consequences too well known to need repetition. These events, in the decade before Hardy's birth, must have added a grimness of tone to the prevailing mood. Inhumanly low wages, poor housing and rising unemployment inevitably fostered a sullen lawlessness.

For desperate men, smuggling and poaching were traditional alternatives to the honest day's work of more conventional employments. When it came to the issue of bare survival there must have been many who – to put it mildly – were no better than they had to be. One of the most telling voices among the labourers whom Hardy drew in his novels is Christopher Coney in *The Mayor of Casterbridge*, saying to Farfrae: 'We be bruckle folk here – the best o'us hardly honest sometimes, what with hard winters, and so many mouths to fill, and God-a'mighty sending his little taties so terrible small to fill 'em with.' As so often with Hardy the penetrating social comment is delivered in the deceptive concealment of dialect comedy. It is Coney who, a few moments later, exclaims, 'For my part I've no more love for my country than I have for Botany Bay!' The contrast with the Scottish sentimentality of Farfrae's songs could hardly be more pointed.

For all their respectability the Hardys also had their contacts with that shadowy world of unobtrusive self-help. In *The Life* Hardy was at some pains to emphasise the gentility of Higher Bockhampton in his childhood, with its retired army and navy officers and its gateposts surmounted with white balls. He did not choose to draw on the early experiences of his grandparents which he had recorded in one of his notebooks. The lonely situation of that first building in the new Bockhampton settlement on the edge of the heath was likely to catch the eye of the smuggling fraternity. It was only a few miles from the coast, with an obscure and thinly populated countryside intervening: as a temporary repository for an illicit consignment of brandy it was ideal. Among the memories of Hardy's grandmother was the sound of a whiplash on the bedroom window-pane in the small hours after midnight. This was the signal for her husband to go downstairs and bring indoors the tubs of brandy deposited on the threshold. These he would hide away in a closet until it was safe for the smugglers to return and collect them.

As other homesteads were built the handling of contraband became too risky and had to end, but at least one of the new neighbours would have been a ready enough accomplice. Mr Kenfield was a guard on the mail-coach from Dorchester to London. He lived near the Hardys in the 1830s, driving his pony and gig into Dorchester to take charge of the coach which used to make a very brief and unscheduled stop at the gate of the plantation separating Higher Bockhampton from the London road. Anyone who observed closely would have seen a youth named John Downton step out and hand up a hamper to the guard before the coach, scarcely pausing, moved on again. On the return journey Kenfield simply threw the empty hamper overboard at the same spot for Downton to carry back through the plantation to Higher Bockhampton. The likely contents of the hamper would have been game bought from the local poachers and items like butter and eggs filched by one of the dairymen, all of which brought the guard a useful second income on London's black market. Once the hamper was safely picked up and stowed away out of sight, the guard could concentrate on his next duty, which was to blow his horn at the entry into Piddletown – as he would have named it – to indicate his readiness to collect mail-bags.

Such are the memories that linger in Veterans' Valley or Cherry Alley, to use the earlier names for the lane that led Hardy's grandparents to New Bockhampton and what is now known as 'Hardy's Birthplace'.

CHAPTER THREE

Egdon Heath

In the neighbouring landscape of Hardy's childhood the two salient features were the Heath and the river Frome. The valley of the Frome separates Dorchester from the settlements of Stinsford and Bockhampton on its northern flank as it flows from its downland sources into the heaths that will march with it to its outfall in Poole Harbour. These heaths – and they are many, individually named – were given by Hardy the collective name of Egdon Heath. In the immediate vicinity of the Hardy homestead were Bhompston Heath, Duddle Heath and Puddletown Heath. They formed the wild background to the New Bockhampton properties:

> The outlook, lone and bare,
> The towering hawk and passing raven share,
> And all the upland round is called 'The He'th'.

This severe, unwelcoming landscape, with its strange beauty and untameable character, became one of the grand metaphors in Hardy's imagination – a symbol of Nature's indifference to human frustration and despair.

> As evening shaped I found me on a moor
> Sight shunned to entertain:
> The black lean land, of featureless contour,
> Was like a tract in pain.

It is clearly the heaths near his home that he describes in that poem, 'A Meeting with Despair'. Indeed the manuscript bears the words 'Egdon Heath', subsequently deleted.

In the famous description of Egdon which forms the opening chapter of *The Return of the Native* Hardy takes the grimness of the scene and, without softening it, gives it a majestic quality. What he emphasises is the brooding darkness, the sombre tones, of the 'obscure, obsolete, superseded country' to which Clym Yeobright will return:

A Saturday afternoon in November was approaching the time of twilight, and the vast tract of unenclosed wild known as Egdon Heath embrowned itself moment by moment. Overhead the hollow stretch of whitish cloud shutting out the sky was as a tent which had the whole heath for its floor.

The heaven being spread with this pallid screen and the earth with the darkest vegetation, their meeting-line at the horizon was clearly marked. In such contrast the heath wore the appearance of an instalment of night which had taken up its place before its astronomical hour was come: darkness had to a great extent arrived hereon, while day stood distinct in the sky. Looking upwards, a furze-cutter would have been inclined to continue work; looking down, he would have decided to finish his faggot and go home. The distant rims of the world and of the firmament seemed to be a division in time no less than a division in matter. The face of the heath by its mere complexion added half an hour to evening; it could in like manner retard the dawn, sadden noon, anticipate the frowning of storms scarcely generated, and intensify the opacity of a moonless midnight to a cause of shaking and dread.

In fact, precisely at this transitional point of its nightly roll into darkness the great and particular glory of the Egdon waste began, and nobody could be said to understand the heath who had not been there at such a time. It could best be felt when it could not clearly be seen, its complete effect and explanation lying in this and the succeeding hours before the next dawn: then, and only then, did it tell its true tale. The spot was, indeed, a near relation of night, and when night showed itself an apparent tendency to gravitate together could be perceived in its shades and the scene. The sombre stretch of rounds and hollows seemed to rise and meet the evening gloom in pure sympathy, the heath exhaling darkness as rapidly as the heavens precipitated it. And so the

25

obscurity in the air and the obscurity in the land closed together in a black fraternization towards which each advanced half-way.

The place became full of a watchful intentness now; for when other things sank brooding to sleep the heath appeared slowly to awake and listen. Every night its Titanic form seemed to await something; but it had waited thus, unmoved, during so many centuries, through the crises of so many things, that it could only be imagined to await one last crisis – the final overthrow.

Hardy's introduction of the word 'waste' is particularly telling. 'The Egdon waste', as he saw it, was part of the waste land that lay outside the reach of civilisation. It belonged to the primeval non-human world. He quotes Leland's description of it as 'overgrown with heth and mosse' and stresses that 'ever since the beginning of vegetation its soil had worn the same antique brown dress'. Man had made no mark on it – at least no agricultural mark.

Another of Dorset's sons, Sir Frederick Treves, took up the same theme in his *Highways and Byways in Dorset*. Here in 1906 he wrote:

The Great Heath is a veritable part of that Britain the Celts knew, since upon its untameable surface twenty centuries have wrought no change. It is a primitive country still. The wheat, the orchard trees, and the garden flowers on its confines are products of civilisation, and are newcomers to the land. Here, still living, are the rough, hardy aborigines – the heather, the bracken, and the gorse.

A third Dorset voice, that of Ralph Wightman who lived at Puddletown, contributed the following picture of the Heath in 1953 in his book *The Wessex Heathland*:

Every inch of the heath is twisted and riven into senseless shapes. There are pits which hold no water and valleys which grow no green pastures. There are hills which give no prospect and brooks which end in a stagnant bog. This is the world when it was 'without form and void'.

Geographically the heathland of south-east Dorset can be defined with reasonable approximation by the following northern and southern boundaries. On the north proceed from Higher Bockhampton (Puddletown Heath) to Briantspuddle, Bloxworth, Lytchett Matravers, Canford, Holt, Cranborne Common and Alderholt; on

Shaftesbury: the western prospect

Godlingston Heath, near Studland

Milton Abbas

Sturminster Newton: footbridge over the river Stour

Sturminster Newton: the Stour below Riverside Villa

Earthworks on Eggardon Hill

The Hardy graves at Stinsford

Shaftesbury: Gold Hill

'Under a leaf-wove awning of green' – the Vallency valley

Sunset on Winfrith Heath

An Egdon rarity: the marsh gentian

North Cornwall: Pentargan Bay

the south from West Knighton to Owermoigne, East Knighton (Winfrith Heath), Wool, Coombe Heath and Bovington Heath (almost to East Lulworth therefore), and then due east along the inland line of the Purbeck hills to Studland, continuing as the coastal hinterland to the river Avon at Christchurch. The valley of the Avon is a convenient boundary to the east, although the same heathy conditions extend beyond the Avon into much of the New Forest.

The link between the Dorset heaths and the New Forest is highlighted in Hardy's poem 'Last Look Round St Martin's Fair', where his attention is caught by the ponies – or 'heathcroppers' to use the picturesque name he gives them:

> The unsold heathcroppers are driven home
> To the shades of the Great Forest whence they come
> By men with long cord-waistcoats in brown monochrome.

'Small, hardy animals of a breed between Galloway and Exmoors' is how Hardy described them. Their descendants would probably be identified today as of the New Forest breed, one of nine recognised British breeds of mountain and moorland ponies. It would have been the general type, if not the pure stock, of the heathcroppers which feature prominently in the natural background of Egdon Heath. As Hardy observes in *The Return of the Native* – 'Egdon was populated with heath-croppers and furze-cutters rather than with sheep and shepherds'. They are images of poverty, of the humble uses to which the heathland vegetation could at best be put. The ponies, uniquely among domestic animals, could pick a living of a sort on the heath. The bundles of cut furze were an acceptable fuel for firing. Occasionally small sectors of such almost worthless land would be set aside for the poor of a parish to gather their own fuel, with less excuse therefore for trespassing elsewhere.

The size of the heathland west of the Avon valley has been estimated for the middle of the eighteenth century as about forty thousand hectares (roughly 100,000 acres). At that time it would have answered more or less to Treves's description of it as 'a veritable part of that Britain the Celts knew'. Hardy commented on the word used in the Domesday Book – Bruaria – to describe the condition of Egdon as a 'heathy, furzy, briary wilderness'; the same word persisted in the survey John Norden made in 1605 for Robert Cecil of the manor of Cranborne, with its references to 'Bruere de

Cranborn' and 'Bruere de Alderholt'. There is no reason to suppose that a further 150 years brought any significant change. Egdon continued to lie outside the bounds of cultivation. In some parts the topsoil was too thin and arid to hold moisture and build up fertility; in others it was ill-drained and marshy, forming stagnant bogs which shivered and quaked; and beneath the surface was the formidable 'iron pan' of solidly impacted sand which defied the spade and the traditional horse-drawn plough.

After 1750 Egdon was looked at more critically by the evangelists of agricultural improvement. The new arable rotations and the general application of a more scientific approach to farming gave a fresh urgency to schemes of land reclamation. The presence of a wilderness became a challenge, and tolerance of its continued existence was almost a moral reproach. Confronting the heathland east of the Avon, William Cobbett exclaimed: 'A poorer spot than this New Forest there is not in all England; nor, I believe, in the whole world. It is more miserable than Bagshot heath.' When Arthur Young considered Egdon Heath his response was characteristic: 'What fortunes are here to be made by spirited improvers!'

When Hardy was born the spirit of improvement cannot have made much progress. To cope with a rising native population there was some new housing encroaching on the heath. New Bockhampton is itself an example of that, but the real impact of urban development did not come until the railways began to operate. Similarly any large-scale breaking of land for forestry or agriculture had to await the later technological developments which have transformed much of Egdon during the present century.

In this, as in so many ways, Hardy is a transitional figure, always sensitive to the tides of change in which he lived; and there is an incident in his childhood which has a particular aptness to the story of Egdon Heath. It is an incident which might seem trivial, but for him it had an enduring resonance. He recalled it in *The Life*; he made it the subject of a poem; and he wove it into the experience of Jude in *Jude the Obscure*. In *The Life* he pictured himself lying on his back in the sun and covering his face with his straw hat. The lining of the hat had disappeared, so 'the sun's rays streamed through the interstices of the straw'. As he lay there, 'reflecting on his experiences of the world so far as he had got, he came to the conclusion that he did not wish to grow up. Other boys were always talking of when they would be men; he did not want at all to be a man'.

In that autobiographical passage there is no indication of where the boy was lying but the picture becomes clearer in the opening verse of the poem, 'Childhood among the Ferns':

> I sat one sprinkling day upon the lea,
> Where tall-stemmed ferns spread out luxuriantly,
> And nothing but those tall ferns sheltered me.

Clearly the child was playing in the bracken on the heath behind his home. The poem goes on to describe how the rain increased and the enclosing fronds of bracken made a sort of miniature house, in which the young Thomas remained securely until the downpour stopped:

> The sun then burst, and brought forth a sweet breath
> From the limp ferns as they dried underneath:
> I said: 'I could live on here thus till death';
>
> And queried in the green rays as I sate:
> 'Why should I have to grow to man's estate,
> And this afar-noised World perambulate?'

This was an experience that Hardy recalled more distinctly than any other of that period. It reflects his deep rootedness in the world of his childhood, to the extent that the heath becomes his personal Eden: to be expelled from it can lead only to sorrow. When he decided to give fuller expression to this emotion in one of his novels, it might be presumed that the boyhood of Clym Yeobright in *The Return of the Native* would be the occasion, since Hardy tells us that

> If any one knew the heath well it was Clym. He was permeated with its scenes, with its substance, and with its odours. He might be said to be its product. His eyes had first opened thereon; with its appearance all the first images of his memory were mingled; his estimate of life had been coloured by it . . .

But Clym regained his paradise. Back home from the 'afar-noised World' he walked on Egdon Heath, savoured the wide prospect 'and was glad'.

It is in *Jude the Obscure* that we find again the image of the boy lying on the ground and looking through his straw hat at the sun. He is now far from Egdon, in North Wessex. There are no bracken

29

fronds and no heather: Jude is lying on a heap of litter near a pig-sty. The atmosphere is more plainly hostile, the boy's feelings are expressed with a bitter vehemence:

> The fog had by this time become more translucent, and the position of the sun could be seen through it. He pulled his straw hat over his face, and peered through the interstices of the plaiting at the white brightness, vaguely reflecting. Growing up brought responsibilities, he found. Events did not rhyme quite as he had thought. Nature's logic was too horrid for him to care for. That mercy towards one set of creatures was cruelty towards another sickened his sense of harmony. As you got older, and felt yourself to be at the centre of your time, and not at a point in its circumference, as you had felt when you were little, you were seized with a sort of shuddering, he perceived. All around you there seemed to be something glaring, garish, rattling, and the noises and glares hit upon the little cell called your life, and shook it, and warped it.
>
> If he could only prevent himself growing up! He did not want to be a man.

This composite formulation of the feelings of the boy who lay among the bracken-ferns and heather of Egdon, looking at the sunshine through the interstices of his straw hat, makes it clear that for Hardy the heath was the womb of his personal history. The changes that the future offered were unwelcome and threatening alterations. Egdon symbolised the aboriginal backward connection, the taproot into the distant past, which was to be such a source of strength in Hardy's writing. In *The Mayor of Casterbridge* he emphasised again the primitive immutability of the heath – 'that ancient country whose surface never had been stirred to a finger's depth, save by the scratching of rabbits, since brushed by the feet of the earliest tribes'. Spiritually it was the home of the outcast, the subversive, the rebel. It was the wilderness, hospitable only to scapegoats. In Hardy's own words, 'Civilisation was its enemy'. Characteristically Michael Henchard chose to go to Egdon to die the death of an outcast.

Nevertheless Time does not stand still; and Hardy knew that the absolute and forthright quality of the landscape he portrayed was being smudged and blurred here and there. Within two years of his

' 'Twas just at gnat and cobweb time'

insistence that the surface of Egdon as Henchard knew it in the 1840s remained unscathed, except by rabbits, Hardy published *The Withered Arm*: in this story he made a comparison between the heath in which the action was set and the heath in 1888 as it had since evolved. The time of the story is prior to the extension of the railway to Dorchester in 1847 but probably not earlier than 1800 since Hardy claims to have known the two women whose story he told. In his description of Gertrude Lodge's ride across the heath Hardy is therefore recording the changes made immediately prior to, and during, his own lifetime:

> Though the date was comparatively recent, Egdon was much less fragmentary in character than now. The attempts — successful and otherwise — at cultivation on the lower slopes, which intrude and break up the original heath into small detached heaths, had not been carried far; Enclosure Acts had not taken effect, and the banks and fences which now exclude the cattle of those villagers who formerly enjoyed rights of commonage thereon, and the carts of those who had turbary privileges which kept them in firing all the year round, were not erected. Gertrude, therefore, rode along with no other obstacles than the prickly furze-bushes, the mats of heather, the white water-courses, and the natural steeps and declivities of the ground.

These later features have no place in the Egdon of the higher flights of Hardy's poetic imagination. They are the reportage of a more humdrum level of social realism. It was no novelty for Hardy to discover that the Ideal and the Real seldom coincide exactly.

If we give Gertrude Lodge's ride a reasonably plausible date around 1825 it is clear that the fragmentation of the heath, though much less marked than in 1888, had already begun. The spirit of 'improvement', exemplified in Arthur Young, was at work and its adherents saw nothing worthy of respect or preservation in the barren waste. If, as Hardy said, 'Civilisation was its enemy' they were wholeheartedly on the side of civilisation as the word was understood in the classical, rational-scientific sense of the eighteenth century. Their philosophy was clearly expressed by a writer with whose work Hardy was certainly familiar — John Hutchins, the Dorset historian. This is how Hutchins described Egdon in 1773:

Near Piddletown begins a large tract of heathy ground, which from thence eastwards occupies a great part of the southern coast, and extends to Hampshire and Surrey, and to the great heaths beyond London. This is professedly the most barren part of the county; and Nature, who has in other parts distributed her beauties with so liberal a hand, seems here, by way of contrast, to exhibit a view of all others the most dreary and unpleasing. It supplies the inhabitants with a cheap fuel, and supports a small breed of sheep, whose flesh is allowed to be sweet and well tasted, and which are not subject to the rot, or *coath*, as it is termed among the shepherds, which in a wet season too often

The ancient face of Egdon: gorse and heather on Studland Heath

infects those that are fed on richer land. It is true of late years many spots have been greatly improved; for which we are chiefly indebted to the skill and taste of James Frampton of Moreton, John Bond of Grange, and Humphry Sturt, esqrs; and Nature, always a friend to industry, has yielded to art. These appear as gardens in the midst of a desert; and with the addition of firs planted in clumps, and now beginning to be dispersed in all parts, meliorate the face of the country.

Humphry Sturt is a particularly interesting figure. Horton tower survives as his most obvious memorial. He enlarged Crichel House and moved the village of Moor Crichel – much as Damer moved Milton Abbas – to create an ornamental lake. Brownsea Island was his, and to improve the fertility there he transported the ashes which were a by-product of London soap factories. This introduction of an artificial fertiliser from an unexpected source was the kind of innovation by this man of adventurous intellect, which earned him the respect and admiration of his contemporaries. It was under the impact of such men that the 100,000 acres of heathland mapped by Isaac Taylor had declined by the end of the Napoleonic Wars to an estimated figure of about 75,000. No doubt this first major phase of reclamation concentrated on the more amenable sectors.

The agricultural improver was a familiar figure to Hardy, who portrayed such a one within the context of Egdon Heath in *The Return of the Native*:

> To many persons this Egdon was a place which had slipped out of its century generations ago, to intrude as an uncouth object into this. It was an obsolete thing, and few cared to study it. How could this be otherwise in the days of square fields, plashed hedges, and meadows watered on a plan so rectangular that on a fine day they look like silver gridirons? The farmer, in his ride, who could smile at artificial grasses, look with solicitude at the coming corn, and sigh with sadness at the fly-eaten turnips, bestowed upon the distant upland of heath nothing better than a frown.

The cultivations which so charmed Hutchins as 'gardens in the midst of a desert' did not always prosper, and there can be no doubt that Hardy's gut-reaction was to ill-wish them. Clym and his author are plainly at one in their 'barbarous satisfaction at observing that, in some of the attempts at reclamation from the waste, tillage, after holding on for a year or two, had receded again in despair, the ferns and furze-tufts stubbornly reasserting themselves'.

At the end of the last century, at about the time therefore of the publication of Hardy's final novel, the surviving area of his native heathland has been put at little more than 55,000 acres. How much of the decline was due to agriculture and afforestation is difficult to gauge. Farming generally was entering a long decline in the last quarter of the century and it was the railways and the urban developers who were now setting the pace of a changing landscape. The coastal development from Boscombe and Bournemouth to Poole spread inland to absorb much of the southern heaths. A secondary railway development in the 1860s, linking Salisbury to West Moors and Wimborne, traversed the impoverished podsol of Verwood and Alderholt and encouraged house-building in what had been a wilderness, apart from the narrow band of clay which supported a pottery industry. With the new system of communications brought by the railroads, land which had been virtually worthless was swallowed up in a development boom. It is a trend which continues to this day with Verwood, for example, projecting itself as a town of 100,000 population by the end of the millennium.

The twentieth-century story of Egdon is one of accelerating dismemberment and suppression, in which two quite separate and distinct forces are at work. One embodies the conviction that the advanced technology of land-reclamation for farming and forestry can bring heathland – like a converted heathen – into the general harmony of a rural economy. The other takes the opposite view, presuming that Egdon should be regarded as irredeemable and given a new destiny as so many parcels of characterless acres, on which a variety of modern installations may be sited without the odium of competing for 'good farming land'.

Of the former there is an instructive example to be seen on Morden Heath. A conifer plantation in the vicinity of Morden Bog is named Parson's Pleasure, for a reason which is explained on a plaque, as follows:

This experiment was designed by Frank Parsons MBE, Chief

Looking westwards over Hartland Moor, near Wareham

Forester at Wareham from 1950 to 1968.

The water-logged heath in this area is one of the worst sites in Europe. The experiment demonstrates a practical way of making it plantable by mechanical drainage and fertilising.

He died in 1968 and this plot is dedicated to his memory.

His response to so daunting a challenge must have been gratifying, and it detracts nothing from his achievement to question whether the best use of Europe's alarmingly dwindling wetlands is to cover them with conifers.

Among developments of the latter kind are the Army's tank training-ground at Bovington and the Atomic Energy Establishment at Winfrith. The Bovington Camp dates from 1916 and is one of the direct consequences of a wartime need. So also were some of the land reclamations which responded to the siege conditions of a maritime blockade. In such circumstances the national need for increased acreage of wheat and young timber overrode questions of cost-effectiveness and long-term suitability.

The southward drift of population completes a picture of

pressure on the area which has destroyed the essential character of 85 per cent of Egdon Heath. What remains is probably no more than 15,000 acres of true heathland, much of it in small lots of 50 acres or less. Expanses exceeding an unbroken area of 250 acres number barely a dozen. It is difficult to think of any Wessex landscape of Hardy's youth which has been more radically transformed.

It is appropriate here to question whether it matters very much. In a small, densely populated country there must be a case for putting every inch of land to good use. In itself that is a proposition which can barely be disputed but its interpretation is fraught with controversy: land which in its natural state is 'worthless' to some may be uniquely valuable to others. Such conflicts of opinion may range from merely personal idiosyncrasies to the measured opposition of contrasting philosophies, and the latter is certainly the case on Egdon Heath. The visual prospect that it offered to Hutchins was 'of all others the most dreary and unpleasing'. His is the voice of eighteenth-century aesthetics: the gothic-romantic answer comes from Hardy. Claiming that Egdon has a 'sublimity' denied to conventional beauty-spots, Hardy continues:

> Fair prospects wed happily with fair times; but alas, if times be not fair! Men have oftener suffered from the mockery of a place too smiling for their reason than from the oppression of surroundings oversadly tinged. Haggard Egdon appealed to a subtler and scarcer instinct, to a more recently learnt emotion, than that which responds to the sort of beauty called charming and fair.

> Indeed, it is a question if the exclusive reign of this orthodox beauty is not approaching its last quarter. The new Vale of Tempe may be a gaunt waste in Thule: human souls may find themselves in closer and closer harmony with external things wearing a sombreness distasteful to our race when it was young. The time seems near, if it has not actually arrived, when the chastened sublimity of a moor, a sea, or a mountain will be all of nature that is absolutely in keeping with the moods of the more thinking among mankind. And ultimately, to the commonest tourist, spots like Iceland may become what the vineyards and myrtle-gardens of South Europe are to him now; and Heidelberg and Baden be passed unheeded as he hastens from the Alps to the sand-dunes of Scheveningen.

37

If Hutchins speaks with the voice of Pope, it is the accents of Wordsworth that echo in Hardy's bold statement of the sublime wilderness-beauty revealed in mountain peaks, barren shores and the 'haggard' heath of his childhood. In his preface to the fifth edition of *Tess of the d'Urbervilles*, in 1892, Hardy made the point that public attitudes may be subtly influenced to take a new direction as the result, not of overt argument, but of 'sentiment' expressed in a novel. In the immediate case of *Tess* it was in the area of social morality, and more specifically of sexual morality, that the novel was influential; but the same principle could be applied to *The Return of the Native* in its influence on the appreciation of landscape. Hardy's prophetic utterance on 'the new Vale of Tempe' gave expression to a sentiment that was gathering strength. When John Wise published *The New Forest: its history and its scenery* in 1862 he set himself as far away as possible from Cobbett's judgment on the Forest by commenting, 'We talk about the duty of reclaiming waste lands and making corn spring up where none before grew. But it is often as much a duty to leave them alone'. And earlier still a voice from across the Atlantic, Thoreau's in *Walden* in 1854, had carried a similar message:

> We need the tonic of wildness – to wade sometimes in marshes where the bittern and the meadow-hen lurk, and hear the booming of the snipe, to smell the whispering sedge where only some wilder and more solitary fowl builds her nest and the mink crawls with its belly close to the ground. At the same time that we are earnest to explore and learn all things, we require that all things be mysterious and unexplorable, that land and sea be infinitely wild, unsurveyed and unfathomed by us because unfathomable. We can never have enough of Nature.

In our own time we have the developing concept that landscapes of exceptional beauty or rarity should be listed in the way that buildings of great architectural or historical value are listed for safeguarding by official controls. Already, designation as what is called 'an Area of Outstanding Natural Beauty' does provide a measure of protection. Where rarity is the criterion, rather than beauty, the designation as 'a Site of Special Scientific Interest' is another and more appropriate form of conservation. In the case of Egdon Heath Christopher Booker, in an article in *The Times*, 20

February 1982, has argued that 'this strange and unique fragment of Britain's landscape is as irreplaceable as a Gothic cathedral' and should be treated accordingly. Meanwhile the designations AONB and SSSI give only a limited and often inadequate protection.

Setting aside for a moment its association with Hardy's novels and poems it is reasonable to consider the other particular reasons for concern about the survival of what remains of Egdon Heath. There are two that stand out clearly. One is the growing desire that our national scenery should be varied enough to include wilderness areas, to retain some contact with the primitive, the aboriginal, the untamed and the undiluted elements in our heritage: it is a desire to experience the whole potential of the natural context within which our lives are set. For our utilitarian purposes we require only a few simplified stereotypes – barbed-wire rectangles of barley, and the like; but these do not meet the deeper needs of the human spirit.

The other factor is the more precise concern of the naturalist who prizes Egdon Heath for the special treasures of its flora and fauna. Common heather, bell-heather and cross-leaved heath are here accompanied by the rare Dorset heath (*Erica ciliaris*). The marsh gentian, one of the loveliest of all our wild flowers, is near the edge of its western range on Egdon Heath and is sadly becoming a great rarity: I have personally seen two of its sites destroyed by building developments, and many others must have been extinguished similarly. The sand-lizard and the smooth snake are two rare British species whose survival is bound up with the type of heathland that is found in south-east Dorset and the adjacent New Forest.

Among birds the raven, so familiar to Hardy in his youth, no longer breeds in the vicinity. Another lost species is the black grouse, which was numerous on the heathland between Ringwood and Wareham in 1782 when John Byng passed that way. On an August day in 1823 the Earl of Malmesbury saw six old blackcocks on Cranborne Common. Malmesbury of Hurn Court, who was an indefatigable sportsman, reckoned to shoot a few blackcock every year up to the mid-1830s. The bird was also plentiful in the New Forest where it was known as the 'heath-poult'. A late shooting record indicates one in 1902 in the Pussex Plantation, on the eastern side of what is now Hurn Airport. Very few can have been seen at any later date and the species has for some time been considered extinct in the area.

Still holding its ground, although against increasing odds, is the Dartford warbler. Principally a bird of the European mainland, the inappropriately named 'Dartford' is at the northern limit of its range on the sandy heathland of southern England. In severe winters its numbers drop alarmingly but it has so far made good its casualties in subsequent breeding seasons. Its greater danger is loss of habitat: it needs the gorse bushes and furzy wildness of Egdon as its ideal breeding-ground.

The key word here is 'habitat'. What makes the Dorset heathland so valuable to naturalists is precisely this intimate combination of geology, climate, soil-structure, vegetation and so forth which provide an ecological context of a character that is becoming increasingly rare in Britain. It is understandable therefore that it is the conservation agencies which are now most active in the defence of Egdon. The Nature Conservancy Council is the arm of official concern: its principal allies among the voluntary organisations are the Royal Society for the Protection of Birds and the Dorset Naturalists Trust, both of which have acquired important areas of heathland. In the face of the authoritative prophecy that those remaining parts of Egdon which are not positively protected will have gone by the year 2000, it may be that the only dependable defence is by purchase or long management-lease.

How very different is all this from 'the He'th' of Hardy's youth! He regarded its existence as eternal. His knowledge of it was not the detailed knowledge of a naturalist but the instinctive commonplace daily familiarity of a countryman. The snake he knew was the adder. The bird that for him most truly represented the atmosphere of Egdon was the nightjar – or 'nighthawk' to give it the name by which he knew it and which he adapted so felicitously to 'dewfall hawk' in the poem 'Afterwards'. That dull-toned monotonous churring sound, so plain and colourless and yet so vibrant with life, coming on a summer evening from nowhere in particular out in the heather and almost suggesting some preposterously large insect, is more evocative of this landscape than any other that Hardy could have conjured up.

A false note intrudes, however, when he feels obliged to insert a learned paragraph on the bird-life of Egdon. The duck-hawk of his boyhood becomes the marsh-harrier, and one can almost hear the turning of pages in the Dorchester Museum Library as he writes:

Feathered species sojourned here in hiding which would have created wonder if found elsewhere. A bustard haunted the spot, and not many years before this five and twenty might have been seen in Egdon at one time. Marsh-harriers looked up from the valley by Wildeve's. A cream-coloured courser had used to visit this hill, a bird so rare that not more than a dozen have ever been seen in England; but a barbarian rested neither night nor day till he had shot the African truant, and after that event cream-coloured coursers thought fit to enter England no more.

A traveller who should walk and observe any of these visitants as Venn observed them now could feel himself to be in direct communication with regions unknown to man. Here in front of him was a wild mallard – just arrived from the home of the north wind.

Looking east over the Nature Reserve and Little Sea on Studland Heath

41

Some of this is plainly nonsense. The coincidence of the numbers of bustards prompts the thought that Hardy misinterpreted the reference to five and twenty of them in 1751 that William Chafin described in his *Anecdotes of Cranborne Chase*. Chafin saw them, not on Egdon Heath and not even in the Chase but east of Salisbury, near Winterslow Hut. Egdon might have seen the occasional bustard but it was never bustard country. It was, and is, better suited to harriers, though not exclusively the marsh-harrier. As for the courser, its recorded appearances in Britain have been as a very rare vagrant visiting impartially most of southern England from Kent to Cornwall and certainly 'creating wonder' wherever it landed. By contrast the mallard that Venn observed, so far from commuting from the high Arctic, was more probably a Wessex resident.

But to return to Hardy's particular cream-coloured courser – this must surely be the one added to the Earl of Ilchester's collection at Melbury in 1853 and noted in 1873–74 in the third edition of Hutchins, where it is stated that the bird was first seen by Lord Digby on Batcombe Down, which is a good day's march from Egdon Heath. The 'barbarian' who shot the bird was Lord Ilchester's keeper, obeying his master's instructions to bag it as a specimen.

What is interesting in this passage is Hardy's indignation at the shooting of the courser. At the time when he was writing it was accepted that the only practicable way of identifying an individual of a rare and therefore unfamiliar species was to shoot it. As in other matters his spontaneous response was ahead of his time.

The Egdon Heath that Hardy evokes for us rests finally not on factual detail but on the impressionist technique which was his particular strength. At his best he takes the simplest materials and distils from them an atmospheric landscape which seizes the reader's imagination with a remarkable and enduring intensity. Egdon Heath is in part a dream world conjured up by Hardy from a residue of early memories which he is able to lift at moments to a visionary level. Some of his most striking effects take the form of sound pictures. The mysterious reappearance of Eustacia on Rainbarrow, with her telescope and her hour-glass, is given its distinctive tone by the weird accompanying sounds of the night wind:

It might reasonably have been supposed that she was listening to the wind, which rose somewhat as the night advanced, and laid hold of the attention. The wind, indeed, seemed made for the scene, as the scene seemed made for the hour. Part of its tone was quite special; what was heard there could be heard nowhere else. Gusts in innumerable series followed each other from the north-west, and when each one of them raced past the sound of its progress resolved into three. Treble, tenor, and bass notes were to be found therein. The general ricochet of the whole over pits and prominences had the gravest pitch of the chime. Next there could be heard the baritone buzz of a holly tree. Below these in force, above them in pitch, a dwindled voice strove hard at a husky tune, which was the peculiar local sound alluded to. Thinner and less immediately traceable than the other two, it was far more impressive than either. In it lay what may be called the linguistic peculiarity of the heath; and being audible nowhere on earth off a heath, it afforded a shadow of reason for the woman's tenseness, which continued as unbroken as ever.

Throughout the blowing of these plaintive November winds that note bore a great resemblance to the ruins of human song which remain to the throat of fourscore and ten. It was a worn whisper, dry and papery, and it brushed so distinctly across the ear that, by the accustomed, the material minutiae in which it originated could be realised as by touch. It was the united products of infinitesimal vegetable causes, and these were neither stems, leaves, fruit, blades, prickles, lichen, nor moss.

They were the mummied heath-bells of the past summer, originally tender and purple, now washed colourless by Michael-mas rains, and dried to dead skins by October suns. So low was an individual sound from these that a combination of hundreds only just emerged from silence, and the myriads of the whole declivity reached the woman's ear but as a shrivelled and inter-mittent recitative. Yet scarcely a single accent among the many afloat tonight could have such power to impress a listener with thoughts of its origin. One inwardly saw the infinity of those combined multitudes; and perceived that each of the tiny trum-pets was seized on, entered, scoured and emerged from by the wind as thoroughly as if it were as vast as a crater.

When Wildeve joins her later he remarks, 'How mournfully the wind blows round us now!' and Hardy continues:

43

She did not answer. Its tone was indeed solemn and pervasive. Compound utterances addressed themselves to their senses, and it was possible to view by ear the features of the neighbourhood. Acoustic pictures were returned from the darkened scenery; they could hear where the tracts of heather began and ended; where the furze was growing stalky and tall; where it had been recently cut; in what direction the fir-clump lay, and how near was the pit in which the hollies grew; for these differing features had their voices no less than their shapes and colours.

Here, as in so many passages, Hardy's genius as a delineator of landscape is revealed in his welding of the literary sophistication of his adult life with the sensory responsiveness of his childhood and youth. His Egdon is composed of finely drawn perceptions of sight and sound, scent and touch. It is as physical to him as another human body that he has learned to love and fear and even hate through the immediacies of his eyes, ears, nose, hands and feet.

The top of Rainbarrow Hill

If something of that primitive spirit still lingers in the landscape of Egdon Heath today it is most discernible perhaps in the vicinities of Winfrith, Wareham, Morden and Corfe. The Arne peninsula, east of Wareham and extending to the shore of Poole Harbour, contains the reserve of the Royal Society for the Protection of Birds: this is the characteristic heathland habitat of the Dartford warbler. Adjoining Arne is Hartland Moor, with the local headquarters of the Nature Conservancy Council at Slepe Farm. The broad stretch of gorse and heather extending to the ridge of the Purbeck Hills is a splendid sight when an atmosphere of distant haze softens the gaunt ruin of Corfe Castle and gives it a remote and legendary quality, as it might be sung of in some old ballad. Surely nowhere in England is so perfectly designed by Nature to provide an impregnable gateway as this steep mound of Corfe set precisely in the one and only gap through the wall of the Purbeck hills. To see it as the background to the unbroken and untamed spaciousness of the heath is an experience to stir the imagination: the centuries seem to fall away.

Not so on Winfrith Heath, where the twentieth century is at its most insistent. Looking northwards from the Tadknoll-Blacknoll road the skyline is dominated by pylons and the buildings of the Atomic Energy Establishment. In the foreground the heath itself is designated a Site of Special Scientific Interest. The light straw colour of dead grass-stems contrasts with the dark green and chocolate brown and deep purple of gorse and heather, touched with patches of gold; and melting in among these broader strokes is a subtle infusion of the bronzes and emeralds of a myriad mosses. Typically one might find a cock stonechat perched on a spray of gorse, flirting tail and wings as if responding to little flashes of electricity. In the direction of Moreton the Frampton obelisk rises above the tree-tops.

In some parts of Morden Heath where the terrain was best suited to the operation of duck-decoys may still be found the pools and bogs that epitomise one of the enduring aspects of Egdon's traditional nature. Elsewhere there are similar discoveries to be made in smaller but sufficiently authentic areas of heath. Although so much has been lost there are still incentives enough for adventurous walkers to find their own versions of the imagery with which Hardy cast his potent spell.

CHAPTER FOUR

The Valley of the Great Dairies

Running through Egdon Heath from west to east, and thus bisecting it, is the river named variously as Froom, Frome or Var: the Ordnance Survey favours *Frome*, Hardy preferred *Froom* but not exclusively. It offers the strongest contrast to the sombre heathland flanks which slope away from the green and glistening bounty of the river valley. Its waters, as Hardy described them in *Tess of the d'Urbervilles*, 'were clear as the pure River of Life shown to the Evangelist, rapid as the shadow of a cloud, with pebbly shallows that prattled to the sky all day long'.

This is an up-beat scene, a landscape of hope and delight. It was here that Tess was courted by Angel Clare, here that she enjoyed the one sustained period of happiness – albeit precarious – in her tragic life. Her first sight of the valley, after she had walked across the heath from Puddletown, 'sent her spirits up wonderfully', and to give expression to her sudden sense of joy she began to sing the *Benedicite*, with its powerful repetitions of 'bless ye the Lord, praise Him and magnify Him for ever!' From the assured touch of its opening words – 'On a thyme-scented, bird-hatching morning in May' – this whole chapter of the book is keyed to a pitch of celebration, confronting the dourness of Egdon on either side with what Hardy calls 'the irresistible, universal, automatic tendency to find sweet pleasure somewhere, which pervades all life, from the meanest to the highest'.

The alterations wrought during a hundred years are predictable and in some particulars are less marked than one might anticipate. Dairy-farming is still the obvious occupation of the rich alluvial flood-plain, although in methods foreign to those used by Dairyman

Crick. The power-supply for mechanical operations is no longer a capstan turned by a solitary horse, and the old 'conjurers' or white witches are barely recognisable in the veterinary surgeons of today. As for the cows, it is their colour rather than their numbers which show the greater change. Hardy speaks of the 'ripe hue of the red and dun kine', indicating probably the Red Devon and Dairy Short-horn breeds: today it is the black and white of the Friesians that catch the eye. There are 430 Friesians on 1200 acres in the vicinity of Norris Mill and Ilsington Farm, which is probably a similar concentration to what Tess would have seen. What has vanished, as a result of machine-milking and the detachment of butter- and cheese-making to factories elsewhere, is the host of dairymaids for whom there is no longer employment. Vanished with them are such delightful scenes as this:

> All the girls drew onward to the spot where the cows were grazing in the farther mead, the bevy advancing with the bold grace of wild animals — the reckless unchastened motion of women accustomed to unlimited space — in which they abandoned themselves to the air as a swimmer to the wave.

In his account of the dairy at Talbothays Hardy noted that 'the milkers formed quite a little battalion of men and maids, the men operated on the hard-teated animals, the maids on the kindlier natures'. It was considered a large unit, milking nearly a hundred beasts. The numbers of men and women are not given but Tess was one of four maids sharing a dormitory, other women lived nearby and there were at least four men. The demobilisation of these battalions has been accompanied by the amalgamation of farms, so that individual farmhouses may have become redundant. The house itself is quite likely to be occupied by people unconnected with farming, and the old working buildings adapted to other purposes or left to deteriorate. Where a traditional dairy-house still stands it will contain distant memories only of that large room, some thirty feet long, over the milk-house, where Tess slept alongside Marian, Retty and Izz, accompanied by 'the smell of the cheeses in the adjoining cheese-loft, and the measured dripping of the whey from the wrings downstairs'.

Of the general prospect of the valley Hardy provided two interestingly contrasted views, Angel Clare's and Tess's. We see it through

Angel's eyes when he returns from a visit to his parents at 'Emminster' (Beaminster) and pauses on 'a detached knoll a mile or two west of Talbothays' – possibly Frome Hill. From here he looks down into 'that green trough of sappiness and humidity, the valley of the Var or Froom'.

> Immediately he began to descend from the upland to the fat alluvial soil below, the atmosphere grew heavier; the languid perfume of the summer fruits, the mists, the hay, the flowers, formed therein a vast pool of odour which at this hour seemed to make the animals, the very bees and butterflies drowsy.

Tess's first impression is in practical terms, comparing the valley with her native Blackmoor Vale and noting that

> The world was drawn to a larger pattern here. The enclosures numbered fifty acres instead of ten, the farmsteads were more extended, the groups of cattle formed tribes hereabout; there only families. These myriads of cows stretching under her eyes from the far east to the far west outnumbered any she had ever seen at one glance before.

When she arrives at the dairy the richness of the scene is embodied in the cows themselves – 'all prime milchers, such as were seldom seen out of this valley'. For a moment Hardy dwells on these symbols of Nature's bounty:

> Their large-veined udders hung ponderous as sandbags, the teats sticking out like the legs of a gipsy's crock; and as each animal lingered for her turn to arrive the milk oozed forth and fell in drops to the ground.

In every detail of the scene Hardy points up the fecundity of the landscape. Looking at it today one recognises the well-breeched prosperity of the farming settlements that border the valley – Kingston Maurward and Stafford House, Ilsington, Woodsford and Moreton, and further downstream Woolbridge Manor. In the changing generations of their histories these have fluctuated between the working headquarters of a great dairy and the dignified residence of land-owning gentry. Moreton, for example, was the home of the agricultural improver mentioned by Hutchins with such admiration, James Frampton. The obelisk that rises among the

trees on nearby Fir Hill was erected in 1786 to commemorate the man. Of his family it is said that, in the twelve generations of Framptons after 1300, the next in line married an heiress on ten occasions.

Woolbridge Manor beside the river Frome

There are, incidentally, two features of present-day Moreton that would have had a particular interest for Hardy. One is the grave of his friend, T. E. Lawrence – 'Lawrence of Arabia'. The other is the unique glass-engravings by Laurence Whistler on the windows of the church.

For his immediate purpose as a novelist Hardy blurred the surroundings of the valley. He is careful not to identify the site of Talbothays Dairy, which is probably a composite portrayal, and his characters reveal no awareness of the neighbouring dairies or their inhabitants. Moreton appears in *Tess* only as the railway station to which the milk is taken – if indeed it is Moreton and not Wool that Hardy had in mind. Moreton still retains its station and the milk still goes directly to London, but not by rail: it travels by road from a local collecting-centre at Milborne St Andrew.

On the level floor of the valley there are no buildings. They are situated on the borders of rising land which merges eventually into

*Sturt's Weir at
Woodsford*

the Heath. Wandering over the grassy plain beside the river Froom
it is easy to recapture the atmosphere in which Tess and Angel
walked together in mutually absorbed delight. On a March morning
when I last visited White Mead, between Tincleton and Woodsford,
the broad level had a relaxed stillness, disturbed only by the river's
gently surprised murmur as it encountered a shallow patch of
gravel, and by the learned conversations in which rooks engage so
assiduously. A solitary snipe got up abruptly and corkscrewed
away.

It is the fuller summer season that Hardy describes so richly, 'the
leafy time when arborescence seems to be the one thing aimed at out
of doors'. The unfolding and straining upwards of plant life is
caught in a single sentence – 'Rays from the sunrise drew forth the
buds and stretched them into long stalks, lifted up sap in noiseless
streams, opened petals, and sucked out scents in invisible jets and
breathings'.

Milking has always meant early rising and it is the landscape of daybreak that Tess and Angel lead us into:

At these non-human hours they could get quite close to the waterfowl. Herons came, with a great bold noise as of opening doors and shutters, out of the boughs of a plantation which they frequented at the side of the mead; or, if already on the spot, hardily maintained their standing in the water as the pair walked by, watching them by moving their heads round in a slow, horizontal, passionless wheel, like the turn of puppets by clockwork.

They could then see the faint summer fogs in layers, woolly, level, and apparently no thicker than counterpanes, spread about the meadows in detached remnants of small extent. On the gray moisture of the grass were marks where the cows had lain through the night – dark-green islands of dry herbage the size of their carcases, in the general sea of dew. From each island proceeded a serpentine trail, by which the cow had rambled away to feed after getting up. . . .

Or perhaps the summer fog was more general, and the meadows lay like a white sea, out of which the scattered trees rose like dangerous rocks. Birds would soar through it into the upper radiance, and hang on the wing sunning themselves, or alight on the wet rails subdividing the mead, which now shone like glass rods.

In his treatment of landscapes Hardy regularly stresses the associations that link the natural scene with human feelings, so that the one reinforces the other. Not only, does he seem to say, are our emotions influenced by our surroundings, but our moods and feelings can highlight some details, and suppress others, in the scenes that surround us. The more closely we look into the Valley of the Great Dairies, the more strongly does it harmonise with the dramatic shifts and tensions of Tess's changing fortunes. The onset of high summer is noted in these terms:

Amid the oozing fatness and warm ferments of the Froom Vale, at a season when the rush of juices could almost be heard below the hiss of fertilization, it was impossible that the most fanciful love should not grow passionate. The ready bosoms existing there were impregnated by their surroundings.

The bosoms of the three other resident dairymaids were filled with an inarticulate and unrequited love for Angel Clare. In the dormitory above the dairyhouse the echoes of the plant-world's 'rush of juices' are unmistakable.

> The air of the sleeping-chamber seemed to palpitate with the hopeless passion of the girls. They writhed feverishly under the oppressiveness of an emotion thrust on them by cruel Nature's law – an emotion which they had neither expected nor desired. The incident of the day had fanned the flame that was burning the inside of their hearts out, and the torture was almost more than they could endure. The differences which distinguished them as individuals were abstracted by this passion, and each was but portion of one organism called sex.

Similarly when Tess was plunged into a mood of depression 'the evening sun was now ugly to her, like a great inflamed wound in the sky. Only a solitary cracked-voiced reed-sparrow greeted her from the bushes by the river, in a sad, machine-made tone.' Even more striking is the correspondence of Tess's guilty feeling of a secret shame with the tainting of the milk by a single foetid plant which has corrupted the sweetness of the pasture. When the whole company forsakes the dairy to walk in line, quartering the mead in search of the offending roots of wild garlic, there is no mistaking the symbolism which identifies Tess as the sinner – in her own eyes – among the hosts of the virtuous. Landscape and inner meaning are as one.

How totally the scene changes when Hardy comes to the sketching of autumn landscapes! By this stage Tess is pledged to marry Angel and is living 'in spiritual altitudes more nearly approaching ecstasy than any other period of her life'. The scenes in which the lovers walk together show the valley in an idyllic character.

> During this October month of wonderful afternoons they roved along the meads by creeping paths which followed the brinks of trickling tributary brooks, hopping across by little wooden bridges to the other side, and back again. They were never out of the sound of some purling weir, whose buzz accompanied their own murmuring, while the beams of the sun, almost as horizontal as the mead itself, formed a pollen of radiance over the landscape.

In autumn the presence of the river is more strongly felt, the sounds of stream and brook become more noticeable. These are the details that now emerge in the landscape as Hardy saw it:

> The water was now high in the streams, squirting through the weirs, and tinkling under culverts; the smallest gullies were all full; there was no taking short cuts anywhere, and foot-passengers were compelled to follow the permanent ways.

The sound and motion of water came into prominence at this season for a severely practical reason also. It was the time when the maintenance and preparation of the water-meadows occupied the attention of the dairymen.

> Men were at work here and there – for it was the season for 'taking up' the meadows, or digging the little waterways clear for the winter irrigation, and mending their banks where trodden down by the cows. The shovelfuls of loam, black as jet, brought there by the river when it was as wide as the whole valley, were an essence of soils, pounded champaigns of the past, steeped, refined, and subtilized to extraordinary richness, out of which came all the fertility of the mead, and of the cattle grazing there.

The channels and patterns of the water-meadows are still in evidence although the classic technique of irrigation is no longer practised. One of the principal channels has been put to a new use, as a carrier of surplus water, to prevent flooding in the town of Dorchester. The 'silver gridirons' of water that Hardy saw have fallen into desuetude, and the art of the 'drowner' is already a lost art. It is probably no exaggeration to say that the term 'water-meadows' has come to mean nothing more than riverside meadows which are sometimes flooded when the river runs high; yet the controlled distribution of water in artificially prepared channels was an important factor in the management of valley pastures until quite recent times. A man skilled in this technique of irrigation was known as a drowner for the obvious reason that he drowned the herbage by inundating it at will. The last drowner in my personal experience was Lennie Harris of Britford, on the Wiltshire Avon just below Salisbury. It was in about 1950 that he explained to me how he turned the water wherever he wanted it to irrigate the meadows on the Earl of Radnor's estate. This is what he said:

You store up the water in the river by means of hatches, and then you cut what we call a 'carriage', which draws the water across the meadow. The carriage is raised above the level of the land. Side-carriers lead the water out of it, so that your carriage starts as wide as a river and gradually dwindles away to nothing. These side-carriers are dug by the drowner, according as to where he wants the water to flow. If he wants to deflect it he puts clots of earth to make a bank. Ideally the water ought to cover every blade of grass in the meadow. You don't achieve that, of course, but a good drowner keeps the water going over the land as evenly as possible.

How long you keep the water on the meadows varies with the season. Winter time you leave it on for a week or a fortnight, so that it deposits mud and silt which fertilises the land. Summertime you just wet the land as the cattle feed it off. If you put on more water than you need you draw off surplus water into low channels which run back into the river again.

My chief concern is the level of the water – deciding when to close hatches and hold water, and when to open and get some water away. You can't call it back once it's gone! You're opening hatches and closing hatches all the time to keep your level just right. You can't judge by local rain – a shower with us may be a downpour higher up the valley.

And never trust the river – don't you trust her! Always have your eye open. If you make a mistake, you can be up all night going round the hatches and putting it right again. There's no doubt drowning is an art, and it has to be learnt. Unfortunately when the big estates broke up, and the river was divided into small parcels, the water meadows were neglected.

The operation of the water-meadows in the Frome valley must have been influenced by the work of George Boswell of Waddock Farm, which is on the northern side of the valley opposite Moreton. In 1779 Boswell published a treatise on the scientific management of water meadows, the significance of which would not have been lost on James Frampton of Moreton and the other forward-looking landowners of the period who created the landscape in which Hardy located Talbothays dairy-farm. The prospect of an 'early bite' would justify the extra labour.

The pattern of water-meadows continued into the upper reaches of the Frome between Dorchester and Maiden Newton. The river's source is at Evershot ('Evershead') in an area which had a special significance for Hardy, who believed that his ancestors had been important landowners at Woolcombe and Frome St. Quintin. Evershot and its Acorn Inn (the 'Sow-and-Acorn') appear in several stories in an incidental way.

A few miles downstream is Maiden Newton ('Chalk-Newton'), which remains notable for throwing up one of those strangely haunting titbits of information that Hardy delighted to record in his notebooks – 'I hear of a girl of Maiden Newton who was shod by contract like a horse, at so much a year'. A more distinguished feature of this large parish was its choir, which had a prominent part in the story 'The Grave by the Handpost':

> The band of instrumentalists and singers was one of the largest in the county; and, unlike the smaller and finer Mellstock string-band, which eschewed all but the catgut, it included brass and reed performers at full Sunday services, and reached all across the west gallery.

In its course from Evershot to Dorchester the Frome passes through what is – even by Dorset standards – quiet country, tightly flanked with downland. Its approach to Dorchester by Poundbury Camp ('Pummery') touches in a detail of the eighteenth-century scene in the narrative poem 'The Burghers':

> Three hours past Curfew, when the Froom's mild hiss
> Reigned sole, undulled by whirr of merchandise,
> From Pummery-Tout to where the Gibbet is.

The fuller stream which leaves Dorchester has meanwhile recruited its tributaries, Sydling Water and the river Cerne. The point at which the traveller passing eastwards through Dorchester becomes aware of the Valley of the Great Dairies is Grey's Bridge. The bridge takes its name from the Greys of Kingston Maurward, whose line of succession terminated when their heiress daughter, Lora, married George Pitt. As a landmark it was frequently mentioned by Hardy, notably in the poem 'Sitting on the Bridge', which suggests that this was a favourite meeting-place for dairymaids and other young women in a flirtatious mood:

55

Sitting on the bridge
　　Past the barracks, town and ridge,
At once the spirit seized us
To sing a song that pleased us —
As 'The Fifth' were much in rumour;
It was 'Whilst I'm in the humour,
　　Take me, Paddy, will you now?'
　　And a lancer soon drew nigh,
　　And his Royal Irish eye
　　Said, 'Willing, faith, am I,
O, to take you anyhow, dears,
　　To take you anyhow.'

But, lo! — dad walking by,
　　Cried, 'What, you lightheels! Fie!
Is this the way you roam
And mock the sunset gleam?'
And he marched us straightway home,
Though we said, 'We are only, daddy,
Singing, "Will you take me, Paddy?"'
　　— Well, we never saw from then,
　　If we sang there anywhen,
　　The soldier dear again,
Except at night in dream-time,
　　Except at night in dream.

Perhaps that soldier's fighting
　　In a land that's far away,
Or he may be idly plighting
　　Some foreign hussy gay;
Or perhaps his bones are whiting
　　In the wind to their decay! . . .
　　Ah! — does he mind him how
　　The girls he saw that day
On the bridge, were sitting singing
At the time of curfew-ringing,
'Take me, Paddy; will you now, dear?
　　Paddy, will you now?'

Grey's Bridge,
Dorchester

For Tess the Valley of the Great Dairies represented an interlude of happiness, even at times of ecstasy, in a life that was otherwise of sombre tone: 'The Rally' is the overall title given to the chapters in the novel which cover the months at Talbothays. For another of Hardy's heroines, however, the Frome had a very different significance and was presented by Hardy in a correspondingly different way. He first established the general scene during a November night of violent storm:

> The moon and stars were closed up by cloud and rain to the degree of extinction. It was a night which led the traveller's thoughts instinctively to dwell on nocturnal scenes of disaster in the chronicles of the world, on all that is terrible and dark in history and legend – the last plague of Egypt, the destruction of Sennacherib's host, the agony in Gethsemane.

This is an epic preparation for a tragic event. We are brought closer to it thus:

> Only one sound rose above this din of weather, and that was the roaring of a ten-hatch weir to the southward, from a river in the meads which formed the boundary of the heath in this direction.

'Shadwater Weir'
on the river Frome

The heath is Egdon. The anonymous river is the Frome. The weir is Shadwater Weir where, in *The Return of the Native*, Eustacia Vye and Damon Wildeve die by drowning. There could hardly be a more vivid example of the widely contrasting treatments that Hardy may give to a landscape. In *Tess of the d'Urbervilles* the Frome valley broadens out to be a world in itself, with Egdon as a barely noticed fringe along its border. In *The Return of the Native* it is the heath that fills the canvas while the river-valley – reduced to anonymity – is compressed until it is no more than a narrow edging to the vast waste of Egdon.

The reality, needless to say, lies somewhere between the two. At the present time anyone who stands to the west of the Tincleton-Woodsford road may find it difficult to recognise the special qualities that Hardy found in Egdon Heath. Conifer plantations and rhododendrons are not in tune with the spirit of prehistory. The Valley of the Great Dairies comes more nearly to one's expectations. It is still a 'vast flat mead' of unchanging purpose, even if methods change:

> The flowery river-ooze
> Upheaves and falls; the milk purrs in the pail;
> Few pilgrims but would choose
> The peace of such a life in such a vale.

CHAPTER FIVE

The Vale of the Little Dairies

When Tess first came in sight of the great dairies of the Frome valley she contrasted them with the little dairies of her native countryside, the Vale of Blackmore or Blackmoor. Size was the first and obvious distinction, but then she noticed also a difference in atmosphere. The Frome valley 'lacked the intensely blue atmosphere of the rival vale, and its heavy soils and scents'. Frederick Treves picked up this characteristic in his reference to 'the enchanting Vale of Blackmore – that valley of the Blue Mist in whose soft shadows will be found the very heart of England'.

The two best vantage points from which to see Blackmore Vale are perhaps Shaftesbury and Bulbarrow. Shaftesbury, 'that mountain-town' as Hardy described it, is perched like an eagle on a crag to command the long perspective to its south and west, to Marnhull and Stalbridge and Lydlinch. Bulbarrow, or indeed any point along the scarp from Okeford to Minterne, marks the dramatic climax of the chalk downs before the plunge into the greensand and clay of the Vale's very different world.

Treves chose the prospect from Shaftesbury's Park Walk:

> The view from the Abbey terrace is across a vast, verdant, undulating valley of the richest pasture land – a plain without a level stretch in it. It ever rolls away into shallow valley and low hill, with now and then a wooded height or the glittering track of a stream. The land is broken up into a thousand fields, fringed by luxuriant hedges. In every hedge are many trees; trees follow every buff-coloured road, and gather around every hamlet or cluster of farm buildings. It is a country of dairies. Everywhere are there cows, for the smell of cows is the incense of North Dorset.

Hutchins, who found the heathland surrounding the Frome such an eyesore, had only praise for Blackmore Vale seen from its southern heights. 'From the neighbouring hills,' he wrote in 1773, 'the frequent inclosures interspersed with villages afford a prospect to the eye beyond description beautiful.' This was the view that appealed to Hardy: 'The secret of Blackmoor,' he wrote in *Tess*, 'was best discovered from the heights around', and his own word-picture of the Vale was sketched from that position:

This fertile and sheltered tract of country, in which the fields are never brown and the springs never dry, is bounded on the south by the bold chalk ridge that embraces the prominences of Hambledon Hill, Bulbarrow, Nettlecombe-Tout, Dogbury, High Stoy, and Bubb Down. The traveller from the coast, who, after plodding northward for a score of miles over calcareous downs and corn-lands, suddenly reaches the verge of one of these escarpments, is surprised and delighted to behold, extended like a map beneath him, a country differing absolutely from that which he has passed through. Behind him the hills are open, the sun blazes down upon fields so large as to give an unenclosed character to the landscape, the lanes are white, the hedges low

Nettlecombe Tout

Melbury Bubb seen from Bubb Down Hill

and plashed, the atmosphere colourless. Here, in the valley, the world seems to be constructed upon a smaller and more delicate scale; the fields are mere paddocks, so reduced that from this height their hedgerows appear a network of dark green threads overspreading the paler green of the grass. The atmosphere beneath is languorous, and is so tinged with azure that what artists call the middle distance partakes also of that hue, while the horizon beyond is of the deepest ultramarine. Arable lands are few and limited; with but slight exceptions the prospect is a broad rich mass of grass and trees, mantling minor hills and dales within the major. Such is the Vale of Blackmoor.

'The fields are never brown and the springs never dry' – the almost liturgical cadence seems to suggest the idyllic pastoral mood of the twenty-third psalm. The linking of pure springs and green pastures as the key to this landscape was the theme of a radio talk broadcast in 1944 by Ralph Wightman:

> The land drops four hundred feet very steeply to the Vale of Blackmore. Immediately at the foot of this very steep chalk slope there is a narrow band of greensand soil, often not more than a few hundred yards wide and never more than three miles. It is full of springs, lovely clear water bubbling out of the base of the hill, inexhaustible and never varying more than a degree or two from a temperature of 54°F. In winter it feels warm, and the mist rises from it on a frosty night, while in summer it is so cold that a glass dipped in it is immediately covered with dew. These deep springs of the greensand water all the wide clay vale.

Shaftesbury and Sturminster Newton might each claim to be regarded as the gateway to the Vale, but with this important distinction: Shaftesbury is a waterless town, whereas Sturminster Newton is couched on the banks of the river Stour. Shaftesbury's stance is that of the aloof spectator, committed in one direction to the Vale of Blackmore but in the other, eastwardly, to the very different world of Cranborne Chase. Sturminster and the Stour are inseparable from each other, the town enfolded in one of the river's winding, wandering bends; and it is the Stour, with its tributaries, which gives the Vale its principal characteristic.

Both towns were important to Hardy. In 1875 he considered renting a cottage in Shaftesbury, but eventually went instead to Swanage. In 1895 one of his letters to Florence Henniker mentioned that a lady-novelist who frequented his London tea-parties 'has come to Shaftesbury on my recommendation of the bracing air. I think it will become a health resort some day'. He similarly emphasised the 'medicinal' virtue of the town's air in his magnificent celebration of Shaston – 'the city of a dream' – which opens the fourth part of *Jude the Obscure*. Here too he describes in unusual detail some of the town's streets and buildings – notably the 'ancient dwelling' in Bimport Street known as 'Old-Grove Place' where Phillotson lived at the time of his marriage to Sue Bridehead. The survival of this name from the sixteenth century is interesting. The

63

first Groves appeared in Shaftesbury in Henry VIII's reign and quickly prospered as lawyers and land-stewards. A map of the town in 1615 shows two houses in Bimport as worthy of individual mention: one is the 'fair turreted house' of Lord Arundell, the other is Mr William Grove's. Subsequently the Groves became big land-owners in the villages east of Shaftesbury with their family seat, Ferne House, in Donhead St Andrew; and it is a strange coincidence that Hardy had scarcely completed the story associated with Old-Grove Place when he met one of the family, Agnes Grove, and formed with her an enduring friendship.

Sturminster Newton has even stronger connections with Hardy for it was here that he spent what he considered to be the happiest years of his married life with Emma. In the summer of 1876 they rented 'Riverside Villa', one of a semi-detached pair overlooking the Stour. A handsomely engraved slate plaque commemorating their tenancy is unfortunately attached to the wrong one of the pair, according to Michael Millgate who appears to have resolved the matter beyond doubt in his biography of Hardy. In front of the villa the land slopes down to the reed-fringed Stour where it is divided

Prospect of the Stour from 'Riverside Villa', Sturminster Newton

by a small island. A short distance upstream is a footbridge, erected in 1841 by J. Conway: its four stone piers with a parapet of ornamental ironwork were a familiar part of Hardy's daily scene. On it he positioned himself in the poem 'On Sturminster Foot-Bridge', listening to the clucking sound of the water and watching the swallows drop down to roost in the withy-beds. In another poem 'The Musical Box' he pictured himself as he 'walked by Stourside Mill, where broad/Stream-lilies throng'. The mill is still in use though it no longer uses water-power; between the mill and the main stone bridge into the town the traces of water-meadows are easy to recognise. The town itself retains much of its older character in its buildings: indeed a visitor to Wessex who sought to recapture the atmosphere of the small market towns that figure so prominently in Hardy's stories would find Sturminster Newton more rewarding than most. Its agreeable jumble of architectural styles, its peaceful back-lanes, and its clustering about a recognisable centre give the town a distinctive atmosphere in the nineteenth-century manner. The familiar preoccupations of country life continue strongly, in support of Hardy's amusing description – 'vegetables pass from growing to boiling, fruit from the bushes to the pudding, without a moment's halt, and the gooseberries that were ripening on the twigs at noon are in the tart an hour later'.

The Stour was a particular source of pleasure to Hardy. In his bachelor days at Weymouth he had enjoyed rowing in the Bay: at Sturminster he could take it up again, as he noted in July 1876:

> Rowed on the Stour in the evening, the sun setting up the river. Just afterwards a faint exhalation visible on surface of water as we stirred it with the oars. A fishy smell from the numerous eels and other fish beneath. Mowers salute us. Rowed among the water-lilies to gather them.

The sunsets were particularly striking at 'Riverside'. On one occasion Hardy wrote: 'This evening the west is like some vast foundry where new worlds are being cast'; and he observed that 'a man comes every evening to the cliff in front of our house to see the sun set, timing himself to arrive a few minutes before the descent. Last night he came, but there was a cloud. His disappointment'.

Another impressive spectacle was the Stour in flood after incessant rain:

Lumps of froth float down like swans in front of our house. At the arches of the large stone bridge the froth has accumulated and lies like hillocks of salt against the bridge; then the arch chokes, and after a silence coughs out the air and froth, and gurgles on.

In the record of his years at Sturminster Newton Hardy has left one other sketch of life there which is worth quoting for its description of girls dancing – much as they dance in *Tess of the d'Urbervilles* after the club walk:

> June 28. Being Coronation Day there are games and dancing on the green at Sturminster Newton. The stewards with white rosettes. One is very anxious, fearing that while he is attending to the runners the leg-of-mutton on the pole will go wrong; hence he walks hither and thither with a compressed countenance and eyes far ahead.
>
> The pretty girls, just before a dance, stand in inviting positions on the grass. As the couples in each figure pass near where their immediate friends loiter, each girl-partner gives a laughing glance at such friends, and whirls on.

While he was living at Sturminster Newton Hardy walked to Marnhull, which he later named as 'Marlott', the village in *Tess of the d'Urbervilles* where the Durbeyfields lived. It is a rather surprising choice since it is so untypical of the villages in this part of Dorset. For one thing it is remarkably large – the largest village in the county and surely one of the largest in all Wessex. It is also difficult to bring into focus: it is nearer to being a federation of detached wards than an organic entity. The church and the Crown Inn form one unit, with the Crown signalling its connection with the novel through the sign of its 'Pure Drop' bar. Another and quite separate section comprises several shops and even a couple of banks; and patient exploration reveals other facets of what Hardy described as a 'long and broken' and 'dispersed' village. Just how, over the centuries, it came to take its present shape is not easy to comprehend.

Opinions of Marnhull differ sharply. After confessing 'I always get lost here and never know which is quite the centre of Marnhull', Monica Hutchings in *Inside Dorset* described it in 1965 as 'a most beautiful village with many good Ham stone houses'. For Sir

The weir and mill at Sturminster Newton

Frederick Treves, however, in 1906 it was 'a disappointing village, prim and stiff, with houses mostly of slate and stone, together with many villas of the Brixton and Camberwell type. It is as little rustic as a place on the edge of the Blackmore Vale could be'.

The claim made for the authenticity of Tess Cottage in Marnhull is undoubtedly put forward in good faith but it hardly bears examination. According to the legendary encounter between Hardy and a gardener, Mr Blake, who was working in the cottage garden, Hardy paused to look at the cottage and in reply to Blake's question 'Can I do anything for you, sir?' answered, 'Oh, no, thank you, I was only looking at where I put my Tess'. Blake recognised Hardy, it is said, because 'he had recently attended a lecture given by him'.

This was in the summer of 1924 when Hardy was eighty-four and customarily made sightseeing or social journeys by car, accompanied by his wife and a chauffeur. He never in his life gave a public lecture. He is unlikely to have been on foot and alone in Marnhull and even more unlikely to blurt out his private business to a chance contact. What is more probable is that the passer-by was looking for a suitable subject for an illustration or a stage-design to represent the Durbeyfield home and explained his purpose in such terms that he unwittingly led Mr Blake to believe, in all honesty, that the speaker was Hardy himself. There was a renewed theatrical interest in *Tess* at this time, not only because of the Dorchester production of Hardy's own dramatisation by The Hardy Players but also because of the British release of the Sam Goldwyn film of *Tess*: the presence in Marnhull of a photographer, artist, lecturer or journalist in search of background material would not be surprising.

To the south-west of Marnhull the road leading down to Kings Mill Bridge, where the Lydden joins the Stour, discloses a fine open view of the Vale as it stretches away beyond Stalbridge and the Caundle villages. The land exhales a sort of drowsy enchantment. Apart from an eighteenth-century silk factory, known now as Factory Farm, there are no memorable landmarks. The minor roads wander from village to village, in which there is no dominant style of building and pubs are surprisingly few. The charm of the countryside as one passes through it is not in this or that detail but in the whole ambience, the leisurely silences and distant drone of remote life. To wander the Vale with no driving purpose is to enjoy a liberation from the urgencies of existence.

Typically the Vale villages are set on rising ground from which they command open views shading into the blue haze. Linking the villages, the roads and droves are often deep-set between grassy banks and many of them display the warning 'Liable to Flood'. The moist clay bed and the meandering streams of the low-lying pastures made the tofts and knaps of the higher ground the sites for human settlement. One is reminded of the Somerset Levels where similarly the villages cluster on gently rising islands above the floods of winter.

Hardy's appreciation of the Vale was given in forthright terms in his preface to *The Woodlanders*, where he claimed that it 'cannot be regarded as inferior to any inland scenery of the sort in the west of England, or perhaps anywhere in the Kingdom'. It must be admitted that the precise identity of Little Hintock remains ambiguous since Hardy shifted his original plan eastwards to avoid giving any possible offence to the Earl of Ilchester, whose ancestral seat, Melbury Park, adjoins Melbury Osmond: Hardy's mother was baptised and married in Melbury Osmond church and it is this village which probably inspired the first version of Little Hintock. But then, as Mrs Dollery said to Barber Percomb, ''Tis such a little small place that, as a town gentleman, you'd need have a candle and lantern to find it'. If it later found itself in the vicinity of Minterne there was no harm done to the essential story. Either way it answered, as any of half-a-dozen villages hereabouts might do, to Hardy's assessment of it as

> one of those sequestered spots outside the gates of the world where may usually be found more meditation than action, and more listlessness than meditation; where reasoning proceeds on narrow premises, and results in inferences wildly imaginative; yet where, from time to time, dramas of a grandeur and unity truly Sophoclean are enacted in the real, by virtue of the concentrated passions and closely-knot interdependence of the lives therein.

To these elements in a drama must be added one more which, in Hardy's view, was attributable to the land itself, the heavy clay soil. In the scene where Tess walks from her winter employment at Flintcomb-Ash to her parents' home at Marlott she enters the Vale in darkness and at once her senses respond to its nature:

The winding road downwards became just visible to her under the wan starlight as she followed it, and soon she paced a soil so contrasting with that above it that the difference was perceptible to the tread and to the smell. It was the heavy clay land of Blackmoor Vale, and a part of the Vale to which turnpike-roads had never penetrated. Superstitions linger longest on these heavy soils. Having once been forest, at this shadowy time it seemed to assert something of its old character, the far and the near being blended, and every tree and tall hedge making the most of its presence. The harts that had been hunted here, the witches that had been pricked and ducked, the green-spangled fairies that 'whickered' at you as you passed; – the place teemed with beliefs in them still, and they formed an impish multitude now.

'Superstitions linger longest on these heavy soils': when he lived at Sturminster Newton Hardy made notes on a farmer who stuck black thorns into the heart of any calf which died, in the belief that this would prevent the disease from spreading; and on a wizard who used to bring little bags containing toads' legs to Bagber Bridge, where they were bought as charms against scrofula. It is a telling stroke of characterisation that makes Tess's mother insist that so potent a volume as *The Compleat Fortune-Teller* should not remain in the house overnight but be lodged in the thatch of the outhouse: much of Tess's life is spent within, and influenced by, a context of portents, conjuring witches, ill-omens and superstitious beliefs. These dark elements are an important thread running through Hardy's writings and there is no doubt that he drew directly from life – from what he heard in the family circle of his childhood and what he later observed. Llewellyn Powys recalled Hardy's description to him of cottagers making the sign of the cross as a raven – that bird of ill-omen – passed overhead.

In *The Woodlanders*, as in *Tess of the d'Urbervilles*, the life of the Vale is patterned with superstitious beliefs and customs. When the foresters and bark-rippers pause to brew up some tea the conversation is 'of the mysterious sights they had seen – only to be accounted for by supernatural agency; of white witches and black witches'; and of a complicated local legend involving two spirits which haunted King's Hintock Court. On old Midsummer Eve the local maidens go into the woods to perform an act of magic at midnight which will reveal their future husbands to them. Most striking of all is John South's belief that the elm outside his dwelling is threatening his life 'every minute that the wind do blow'. As his daughter Marty explains to Dr Fitzpiers:

> 'The shape of it seems to haunt him like an evil spirit. He says that it is exactly his own age, that it has got human sense, and sprouted up when he was born on purpose to rule him, and keep him as its slave. Others have been like it afore in Hintock.'

The deepening human relationships with the trees and with the whole natural scene of the Vale is a constant theme. When Marty is planting young pine trees with Giles Winterborne she sees them as sharing her world with her:

> 'How they sigh directly we put 'em upright, though while they are lying down they don't sigh at all,' said Marty.
> 'Do they?' said Giles. 'I've never noticed it.'
> She erected one of the young pines into its hole, and held up her finger; the soft musical breathing instantly set in, which was not to cease night or day till the grown tree should be felled — probably long after the two planters had been felled themselves.
> 'It seems to me,' the girl continued, 'as if they sigh because they are very sorry to begin life in earnest — just as we be.'

In autumn Hardy describes a walk through the Hintock plantations thus:

> They went noiselessly over mats of starry moss, rustled through interspersed tracts of leaves, skirted trunks with spreading roots whose mossed rinds made them like hands wearing green gloves; elbowed old elms and ashes with great forks, in which stood pools of water that overflowed on rainy days, and ran down their stems in green cascades. On older trees still than these, huge lobes of fungi grew like lungs. Here, as everywhere, the Unfulfilled Intention, which makes life what it is, was as obvious as it could be among the depraved crowds of a city slum.

To the little community of the Hintock villages the trees among which they lived could have different values for different people. Some valued the great trunks for their timber, some wanted the bark for tanning; the coppice wood went for hurdles and thatching spars, the brushwood as faggots for firing; and the cider-maker wanted the fruit of the apple-orchards. Cider had been a particular feature in the eighteenth century when Hutchins praised the Vale as 'profitable for breeding and fatting black cattle, and supplying its inhabitants with cider from their orchards scarce inferior to the produce of the more western counties'. Orchard and timber plantation were interspersed in the Hintocks but the emphasis on orchards increased to the eastward. When Mr Melbury and his daughter Grace were driving home along the western flank of the Vale they looked across a wide district, 'differing somewhat in feature and atmosphere from the Hintock precincts'.

It was the cider country more especially, which met the woodland district some way off. There the air was blue as sapphire — such a blue as outside that apple-region was never seen. Under the blue the orchards were in a blaze of pink bloom, some of the richly flowered trees running almost up to where they drove along.

Today you may find a farmhouse cider-maker here and there, but in the main the traditional drink of the west country has been industrialised in large-scale production. In the second half of this present century many of the small individual orchards attached to a farm have been grubbed up and put to other uses. Where old orchards are renewed the tendency is to operate a contract with a cider factory which provides newly developed dwarf stocks that are more easily harvested.

Hardy saw the areas of woodland beginning to shrink but he had no misgivings about the future of cider. His father made his own and Hardy celebrated it among the 'great things' of life — ranking it with love and dancing.

Sweet cyder is a great thing,
A great thing to me,
Spinning down to Weymouth town
By Ridgway thirstily,
And maid and mistress summoning
Who tend the hostelry:
O cyder is a great thing,
A great thing to me!

In 1873, the year before his marriage, Hardy assisted his father for the last time in the annual cider-making, a task he had always enjoyed from childhood. It is evidently a childhood memory that appears in *Desperate Remedies* when Mr Springrove is making his cider:

> It was about the middle of the early apple-harvest, and the laden trees were shaken at intervals by the gatherers; the soft pattering of the falling crop upon the grassy ground being diversified by the loud rattle of vagrant ones upon a rail, hen-coop, basket, or lean-to roof, or upon the rounded and stooping backs of the collectors – mostly children, who would have cried bitterly at receiving such a smart blow from any other quarter, but smilingly assumed it to be fun in apples.
>
> Under the trees now stood a cider-mill and press, and upon the spot sheltered by the boughs were gathered Mr Springrove himself, his men, the parish clerk, two or three other men, grinders and supernumeraries, a woman with an infant in her arms, a flock of pigeons, and some little boys with straws in their mouths, endeavouring, whenever the men's backs were turned, to get a sip of the sweet juice from the vat.

In Hardy's Wessex cider was the everyday drink. Mr Melbury, sitting at home, had 'a pitcher of cider standing on the hearth beside him, and his drinking-horn inverted upon the top of it'. In the woodlands, during tree-barking, a milking-pail of cider stood near, with a half-pint cup floating on it, for anyone to dip and drink when passing. At the timber auction, similarly, the auctioneer provided milking-pails of cider for his bidders to dip into. On the farms it was customary for each labourer to set down his empty costrel at the farmhouse door at the end of the day, when it was filled for him to collect next morning. At times of exceptionally heavy labour, particularly at harvest time, the daily issue of cider would be increased.

It was not only a common drink. Hardy adds an expert touch of connoisseurship to the description of the hogshead of fine cider 'bought of an honest down-country man' that Miller Loveday, in *The Trumpet-Major*, tapped for his son's wedding:

> It had been pressed from fruit judiciously chosen by an old hand – Horner and Cleeves apple for the body, a few Tom-Putts for colour, and just a dash of Old Five-corners for sparkle – a

selection originally made to please the palate of a well-known temperate earl who was a regular cider-drinker, and lived to be eighty-eight.

In the Vale of Blackmore, as elsewhere, there were those who owned their own cider-mill and press – as well as their own orchard – and could carry through the whole operation. There were others who might have a sufficient orchard but relied on an itinerant cider-maker to bring his appliances and his skill to the task. Such a one was Giles Winterborne in *The Woodlanders*. According to the season he might be making hurdles, or planting trees with Marty South, or helping Mr Melbury with the timber trade; but in the autumn he would assuredly be on the road, accompanied by his servant Creedle, with a pair of horses pulling his mill and press from farm to farm, as he was doing when Grace Melbury met him by chance in the vicinity of High Stoy:

> He looked and smelt like Autumn's very brother, his face being sunburnt to wheat-colour, his eyes blue as corn-flowers, his sleeves and leggings dyed with fruit-stains, his hands clammy with the sweet juices of apples, his hat sprinkled with pips, and everywhere about him that atmosphere of cider which at its first return each season has such an indescribable fascination for those who have been born and bred among the orchards.

She is to think of him later as the fruit-god and the wood-god in alternation – 'sometimes leafy and smeared with green lichen, as she had seen him amongst the sappy boughs of the plantations: sometimes cider-stained and starred with apple pips'. He seems to incarnate a legendary Green Man, symbolising the fertility of the Vale of the Little Dairies. He is the image that Hardy set in a stanza of the poem 'Shortening Days at the Homestead':

> Who is this coming with pondering pace,
> Black and ruddy, with white embossed,
> His eyes being black, and ruddy his face,
> And the marge of his hair like morning frost?
> > It's the cider-maker,
> > And appletree-shaker,
> And behind him on wheels, in readiness,
> His mill, and tubs, and vat, and press.

*The Manor House
at Melbury Bubb*

He comes no more to Stourton Caundle or Henstridge Ash, to Fifehead Magdalen or Melbury Bubb. The forces of change subtract as much as they add, but some things are little changed. The holdings are still small, ranging from 50 acres to 200; and it is still dairying country. The pastoral nature of the land is not to be denied. In the words of a farmer at Holwell – 'plough it and you might get a crop, or you might get nothing'.

Those who mourn the passing of Merrie England may care to note two innovations. Man-traps, such as Timothy Tangs operated, are no longer used. And the *Western Gazette*, in reporting next week's events at West Stour, is unlikely to provide a paragraph to match this from an earlier issue – 10 October 1869 – which Hardy perhaps noticed:

> This village has been, on several evenings recently, the scene of some very disgraceful demonstrations. A crowd of men, women and children have made night hideous with screams, shouts, the rattling of old tin vessels, and the parading of effigies through the streets. The disturbances were brought to a close with the burning of the figures of the obnoxious parties. Wife-beating, especially when indulged in by one who, from his position in the parish, ought to be an example to others, is disgraceful and indefensible, but every sensible person must deprecate such a barbarous mode of censuring the crime as that which is resorted to in rural districts.

CHAPTER SIX

Lyonnesse

When Hardy alighted at Launceston railway station in March 1870, in the course of his architectural work, he was about to enter what for him might be described as almost a foreign country. Unlike the central and eastern parts of his literary kingdom, where the plain light of realism was seldom obscured for long, the west was illumined by the glittering, enticing, disturbing and sometimes confusing light of a romantic vision. Historically and geographically the high moors and towering sea-cliffs of the Devonian-Cornish peninsula have a separate identity. To draw the line of a precise frontier is scarcely to be attempted, but Taunton and Exeter suggest themselves as gateways to a pristine land where our most ancient legends retain their vitality and the successive immigrations from the European mainland hesitated.

In any traveller's experience that dramatic upward sweep west of Exeter is a moment to savour, echoing the even steeper ascent on the northern coast from Porlock to the heights of Exmoor. It is on the western moors – Dartmoor, Exmoor and Bodmin Moor – that the distancing of one's self from the familiar downland of Dorset and Wiltshire is most keenly felt. It is a distance to be measured, not in miles, but in the whole rich texture of one's immediate senses and the long memories of history. If the murmured words *Celt* and *Briton* seem to add something, so much the better. The very soil here is some of the oldest in England.

Among the hordes of summer holidaymakers streaming down the motorway to Cornwall there can be few who are not impelled by some romantic notion of their own, compounded of pixies, poetic legends, saints with quaint names, idyllic fishing villages and clotted cream. They follow a strong tradition, which Hardy epitomises in his own terms:

> What would bechance at Lyonnesse
> While I should sojourn there
> No prophet durst declare.

His choice of the old name *Lyonnesse* sets the mood at once – a mood of expectation, of a readiness to surrender to the powerful magic of a demiparadise. What did in fact 'bechance' on that first visit made so lasting an impression on him that the 'magic in my eyes', with which he returned, remained undimmed to the end of his life. For him, as for so many, Lyonnesse was to be enshrined as the romantic contrast to that workaday world to which each pilgrim must return, haunted thereafter perhaps as Hardy was by 'the opal and the sapphire of that wandering western sea'.

From Launceston, on that first visit, Hardy had a sixteen-mile drive in a dog-cart to St Juliot rectory. In a terse note jotted down at the time he described the drive over the hills as 'dreary yet poetical': next morning he looked out on an 'austere grey view of hills'. His first sight of the sea came later. His first impression meanwhile was of an austere greyness in which he recognised a poetical quality. It was this poetical element which he later identified as the prophetic message that the wind carried to him as he made his journey. In one of the most dramatic of his Cornish poems, 'The Wind's Prophecy', he looks backward repeatedly to her whom he believes to be his true love, awaiting his return, only to be contradicted at each stage by the voice of the wind proclaiming that he is just about to meet his true love for the first time – that she is not dark, as he believes, but fair; not dwelling in the east, but the west; not to be found in a city but beside the ocean. And as a companion-piece to this account of a man caught up in the full force of his destiny he wrote 'A Man Was Drawing Near to Me', in which Emma is shown as similarly unaware of the mounting significance of each landmark that the approaching architect passes – Otterham, Tresparret Posts, Hennett Byre – until the moment comes when

> There was a rumble at the door,
> A draught disturbed the drapery,
> And but a minute passed before,
>   With gaze that bore
>   My destiny,
> The man revealed himself to me.

From that first moment, Lyonnesse carried the most powerfully romantic emotional force for Hardy, and indeed no less for Emma. The days passed at two widely separated levels. There was the practical task of planning the restoration work on the church, discussing the business arrangements with the rector, visiting a slate quarry to select suitable tiles for the roof, and kindred activities. In parallel with these superficial responsibilities went the ardours of a headlong courtship, irradiated with the enchantment of the Cornish scene. Looking back in 1895, in his preface to *A Pair of Blue Eyes*, Hardy spoke of the shore and country about Boscastle (alias 'Castle Boterel') as being for him a region 'of dream and mystery'. He continued:

The coast, north of Beeny to Cambeak

> The ghostly birds, the pall-like sea, the frothy wind, the eternal soliloquy of the waters, the bloom of dark purple cast, that seems to exhale from the shoreward precipices, in themselves lend to the scene an atmosphere like the twilight of a night vision.

*Cornish clifftops
from Rusey
towards Boscastle*

It was in such terms that he responded, consistently and enduringly, to the north coast of Cornwall. The gaunt sheer cliffs and
the violence of the Atlantic breakers impressed him particularly —
so different from Weymouth Bay, where he was accustomed to
swim or row a boat, morning or evening as his fancy dictated. Here
in Cornwall

> From tides the lofty coastlands screen
> Come smitings like the slam of doors,
> Or hammerings on hollow floors,
> As the swell cleaves through caves unseen.

In another poem, 'The Discovery', he speaks of 'Waves like distant cannonades that set the land shaking'. In August 1872 he made
some notes on Beeny cliff as he looked seawards to a dark grey ocean
and recorded 'a lather of foam round the base of each rock. The sea
is full of motion internally, but still as a whole. Quiet and silent in
the distance, noisy and restless close at hand'.

What to Hardy was a novelty had become for Emma an everyday
scene since she settled at St Juliot rectory in 1868, when her sister
married the rector. She had no romantic illusions about what she
called 'the primitive inhabitants', with their belief in witchcraft and
their 'evil-speaking'. More charitably she observed that 'hard

79

labour upon the stony soil made a cold, mostly ill-natured working class, yet with some good traits and fine exceptions'. Her deepest pleasure was found in the countryside itself, the everchanging seascapes and the rearing, precipitous cliffs and hills. She was an accomplished and intrepid horsewoman, responding with the exuberance of youth to the challenge of this rugged terrain. Writing her reminiscences towards the end of her life, she described herself in those distant days at St Juliot:

> scampering up and down the hills on my beloved mare alone, wanting no protection, the rain going down my back often and my hair floating on the wind . . . Fanny [her mare] and I were one creature, and very happy both of us . . . The villagers stopped to gaze when I rushed down the hills. A butterman laid down his basket once to exclaim loudly for no one dared except myself to ride in such wild fearless fashion. Sometimes I left Fanny and clambered down to the rocks and seal caves.

In the presence of the sea itself Emma recognised its power 'to awaken heart and soul'. She revelled in the spectacle of 'the wild Atlantic ocean rolling in with its magnificent waves and spray, its white gulls and black choughs and grey puffins, its cliffs and rocks and gorgeous sunsettings sparkling redness in a track widening from the horizon to the shore'.

Today the gulls are numerous enough and it is possible to see a few puffins in the vicinity of Boscastle, but we can no longer share with Emma the sight of choughs on this coast or indeed anywhere in Wessex. The extinction of the chough as a breeding species in the south-west peninsula is particularly regrettable as it was the county emblem of Cornwall. The last pair lingered on until 1967 in the Duchy. On the neighbouring coast of Devon the chough ceased to breed after about 1910.

Visiting Tintagel in the mid-1790s W. G. Maton observed that the chough was so common on the Cornish coast that it was generally known as 'the Cornish daw'; and he added that 'the natives are so much attached to them that it is very common to see tame ones in their gardens'. He saw considerable numbers flying at Tintagel and described the bird as 'immediately distinguished from the common crow by its red legs and bill'. Fifty years earlier Richard Pococke spoke of 'jays with red bills and legs, called a Cornish jay'. Earlier

St Juliot's Church, restored by Hardy

still, in 1695, Celia Fiennes stayed with a Cornish relative who invited her to extend her visit in order to hear 'the Cornish nightingales as they call them'. She quickly understood that this nightingale was a comic name for the Cornish chough – 'a sort of jackdaw, if I mistake not, a little black bird which makes them a visit about Michaelmas and gives them the diversion of the notes, which is a rough sort of music not unlike the bird I take them for, so I believe they by way of jest put on the Cornish gentlemen by calling them nightingales'.

Tintagel

As a compensation for the loss of the chough the modern visitor to the shores of Emma's recollections will find there a bird she never saw. This is the fulmar, in James Fisher's graphic phrase – the 'grey ghost glider of stormy seas'. The first breeding record for the fulmar in south-west England was in 1944 on the island of Lundy and the bird has since become a familiar sight along the Cornish coast; its seemingly effortless gliding and planing and tacking make a thrilling spectacle.

Seals are still to be found in the caves that Emma would have known. A brief excursion from Boscastle in a fishing-boat will reveal a typical cave in Beeny Cliff, for instance. The face of the cliff, incidentally, is owned by the Galahad Trust, a recent venture sponsored locally with the aim – according to one of its members – of saving Beeny from the National Trust.

Seen from the sea Beeny appears as a broad cliff-face extending from the dark inscrutable inlet of Pentargan Bay to the savagely exposed and eroded face of Buckator that rises above Gull Island. The rock precipice of Beeny is predominantly of dark slate with intrusive beds of a creamy-coloured granite spar. The top frontage carries gorse and heather interspersed with clusters of thrift, or sea-pink, and sea-campion. These upper levels lean back to an inland plateau of meadows grazed by cows and sheep. To the unprejudiced eye it must appear typical rather than distinctive. As Hardy himself pointed out in *A Pair of Blue Eyes*, 'Haggard cliffs, of every ugly altitude, are as common as sea-fowl along the line of coast between Exmoor and Land's End'. Yet among them all it is the 'Cliff without a Name' in that novel – identified later as Beeny – which exemplifies so vividly what Hardy meant when he wrote that 'the beauty of association is entirely superior to the beauty of aspect', or when he commented on Turner's water-colours – 'each is a landscape *plus* a man's soul'. In this connection it is no mere fancy to associate together Hardy's picture in prose and verse of Beeny with Turner's of Boscastle Harbour. Where else on the coast of Britain has such imaginative power been concentrated?

In *A Pair of Blue Eyes* the most graphic portrayal of Beeny begins with Emma's walk along the course of the little rivulet which falls as a cascade into the sea at Pentargan, on the south-western flank of Beeny. It is here that Knight meets her in the well-known scene when he nearly falls to his death over the precipice.

The composition of the huge hill was revealed to its backbone and marrow here at its rent extremity. It consisted of a vast stratification of blackish-gray slate, unvaried in its whole height by a single change of shade.

It is with cliffs and mountains as with persons; they have what is called a presence, which is not necessarily proportionate to their actual bulk. A little cliff will impress you powerfully; a great one not at all. It depends, as with man, upon the countenance of the cliff.

The crest of this terrible natural façade passed among the neighbouring inhabitants as being seven hundred feet above the water it overhung. It had been proved by actual measurement to be not a foot less than six hundred and fifty.

That is to say, it is nearly three times the height of Flamborough, half as high again as the South Foreland, a hundred feet higher than Beachy Head – the loftiest promontory on the east or south side of this island – twice the height of St Aldhelm's, thrice as high as the Lizard and just double the height of St Bee's . . . And it must be remembered that the cliff exhibits an intensifying feature which some of those are without – sheer perpendicularity from the half-tide level.

In the novel Hardy turns Beeny to his professional purpose as the setting for two important incidents in the telling of his story, but the autobiographical overtones are unmistakable. The fictitious lovers who walk and talk on the cliff-top in his pages spring easily and clearly from the deeply felt emotion that he recalled in the poem, 'In Front of the Landscape':

Also there rose a headland of hoary aspect
      Gnawed by the tide,
Frilled by the nimb of the morning as two friends stood there
      Guilelessly glad –
Wherefore they knew not – touched by the fringe of an ecstasy
      Scantly descried.

It was his pleasure with Emma to sit at their ease on Beeny, looking out to sea or making sketches. They were both amateur artists, with pencil or water-colours. In the Dorset County Museum is preserved one such drawing made by Hardy in the summer of

Beeny Cliff

1870 when he visited St Juliot for the second time: it portrays Emma on Beeny, looking somewhat bedraggled since it evidently came on to rain before Hardy completed his drawing. His inscription reads 'Beeny Cliff in the Rain – Aug 22, 1870. "It never looks like summer." E.L.G. (on Beeny)'.

The initials are Emma's (Emma Lavinia Gifford) and hers therefore are the words Hardy quotes. The casual humorous remark, 'It never looks like summer', was one of those sayings that take on a special lustre from being uttered in the intimacy of lovers. At such times some commonplace phrase or simple jest may be seized with a plangency which, though it be inexplicable, is not to be gainsaid. So it was in this instance, with the words implanting themselves deeply in Hardy's mind. Perhaps they became a catch-phrase of the sort that intimate friends or members of a family develop. Many years later they recurred to him in the aftermath of Emma's death:

'It never looks like summer here
      On Beeny by the sea.'
But though she saw its looks as drear,
      Summer it seemed to me.

It never looks like summer now
      Whatever weather's there;
But ah, it cannot anyhow,
      On Beeny or elsewhere!

Nor was it only the words that lingered in his memory. Each detail of the scene was recaptured in two more poems. In 'Why Did I Sketch' he reflects that Emma's death had changed the picture into 'a wordless irony': better to have concentrated on the stark and stiff escarpments of rock and omitted the soft curves of a woman's silhouette. In 'The Figure in the Scene' he virtually translated his picture into verse, tracing again Emma's posture and the rain falling on the cliff:

It pleased her to step in front and sit
      Where the cragged slope was green,
While I stood back that I might pencil it
      With her amid the scene;
            Till it gloomed and rained;
But I kept on, despite the drifting wet
      That fell and stained
My draught, leaving for curious quizzings yet
      The blots engrained.

And thus I drew her there alone,
      Seated amid the gauze
Of moisture, hooded, only her outline shown,
      With rainfall marked across.
            – Soon passed our stay;
Yet her rainy form is the Genius still of the spot,
      Immutable, yea,
Though the place now knows her no more, and has known her not
      Ever since that day.

It is indeed the case that Emma was always to remain for Hardy 'the Genius still of the spot'. Of all his Wessex landscapes the north

Cornish coast stands apart in its impassioned absorption in the woman he loved: so much so that it is difficult to see it in any other terms. Here she was his constant companion, his 'West-of-Wessex girl' whom he visited at intervals; and it was her liveliness of temperament which gave a piquant and memorable novelty to the events of the day.

The countryside they explored together is less altered than many other parts of Wessex. It has taken the colour and style of the twentieth century without conspicuously startling innovations. Its dairy-farming has found a new but unobtrusive focus in the cheese factory at Davidstow. The Penpethy quarry that Hardy visited 'with a view to the church roofing', as he noted in his journal, is no longer in operation; but the quarrying of slate remains an active industry in the neighbourhood. As long ago as the 1540s Leland noted in his *Itinerary* that the cliffs between Stratton and Padstow have 'good fyne blew slates, apte for Howse Kyvering'. Certainly if the nature of the land here had to be characterised in two words they would be *slate* and *granite*. In its origins it was the volcanic heat of the granite of Bodmin Moor which transformed the surrounding masses of Upper Devonian sandstone into slate. Today, as in 1870, Bodmin Moor has a peculiar stark austerity of its own. Brown Willy and Row Tor have little in common with High Stoy or Bulbarrow.

The place to see a slate quarry in operation is Delabole. There is a continuous record of quarrying here since Tudor times. Passing through the district in 1695 Celia Fiennes noted at 'Bole' the existence of 'remarkable quarries for a black stone, exceeding hard and glossy like marble, very durable for pavements. This they send to all parts in time of peace, and London takes much of it'. It was shipped from Barnstaple. A hundred years later the Salisbury doctor, W. G. Maton, recounting his tour of the West, wrote: 'There are quarries, called Denyball slate-quarries, to the left of the Camelford road, that produce an excellent slate for roofs, equal perhaps to any in the Kingdom. Its colour is a greyish blue. The rough masses are raised from their beds by wedges, driven by bars of iron, and are split by means of a strong, broad chisel and a mallet.'

Delabole quarry today is an astonishing sight. The top perimeter, the brim, is a circuit of three miles: the depth five hundred feet. It is a prodigious hole, with a zig-zag road twisting through hairpin bends to the bottom. Seen from the top the earthmoving vehicles below look like children's toys.

The complex includes a museum which displays the history of the industry and some of its industrial archaeology. A craftsman demonstrates the art of splitting slates in the traditional manner described by Maton. The mallet used for the purpose is known as a 'bettle' — a word which in other parts of Wessex sometimes becomes misleadingly a 'beetle'. The grading of slates by size starts with 'Queens, Princesses, Duchesses, Marchionesses' and so on down the scale to conclude with 'Ladies and Small Ladies' — a touch of class that Hardy would have observed with interest.

St Juliot no longer has its individual rector. Its rectory has passed into private hands and the church is served from outside the parish as one of a group of churches. Such life as it had seems to be ebbing away, and it is the dead who sustain it: the churchyard is where its heart still beats. The literary pilgrims who come here, like the woman from Plymouth and the man from Dorchester commemorated on its walls, are transient aliens in the presence of Hepzibah Lillicrap and her neighbours lying in the natural possession of their last resting-places. It is in the churchyard of St Juliot that the temptation to linger is strongest, where ancient stone crosses and slabs of local slate express an enduring continuity, meliorated with the ephemeral tenderness of the Maytime flowers. Few places have such a poignant sweetness and serenity as this churchyard on a spring morning, with cloud and blue sky alternating, and the light changing in easy gradations; with rooks busily attending to family matters overhead, and on every side the mingling colours of red campion and bluebell among many lesser blossoms.

Inside the church the three memorial plaques on the north wall have a closer unity than the casual observer might realise. After an interval of over fifty years they reunite in stone lettering the four principals in that encounter in 1870 which for Hardy was to prove so momentous. The first commemorates the Revd. Caddell Holder, who died in 1882, having been rector of St Juliot when Hardy first visited him to discuss the planned restoration of the fabric of the church. Holder's plaque was erected by Helen, his widow. Helen's sister, Emma Hardy, is the subject of the second plaque, commissioned and supervised by Hardy in 1913 after he had made a carefully measured drawing of the Holder plaque in order to match it. The third one, of Hardy himself, was similarly planned by him in instructions he left to be carried out after his death. Its presence, matching Emma's in every detail, manifests his desire to renew their association in this the first and most romantic setting of their love.

From the church of St Juliot and its erstwhile rectory the lie of the land inclines to Boscastle along the course of the Vallency river – the little brook, of Leland's description, running by the west side of the town and going into the Severn Sea between two hills where it makes a poor haven, in his words 'of no certaine salvegarde'. The inner harbour is now well protected but the narrow inlet is so walled about by cliffs that it is almost hidden from the view of any passing craft which is not positively seeking it. There are still fishing-boats working out of Boscastle, principally for lobster and mackerel.

Leland named it as Botreaux Castle, commonly called Boscastel;

The Vallency river flows into Boscastle harbour

and he explained that the Lord Botreaux was lord of this town, a man of an old Cornish lineage. Hardy's designation 'Castle Boterel' is therefore a revival of the old name rather than the invention of a new one. Leland's condemnation of the place as 'a very filthy Toun and il kept' was not shared by Maton, centuries later, who admired its 'highly romantic situation', with its cottages 'all in a deep valley washed by a small inlet of the sea, whilst fine mountainous eminences crowd round them on all sides, cut by craggy gaps, and clad with brushwood'.

That description of Maton's is true enough today, if one adds the inevitable concomitants of tourism. By contrast with Tintagel's tawdriness, Boscastle retains much of its picturesque and romantic character. To walk the length of the little river from St Juliot to Boscastle Harbour is to share, in reasonably comparable terms, the pleasure implicit in Emma's words:

> Often we walked to Boscastle Harbour down the beautiful Vallency valley where we had to jump over stones and climb over a low wall by rough steps, or get through a narrow pathway, to come out on great wide spaces suddenly, with a sparkling little brook going the same way, in which we once lost a tiny picnic-tumbler, and there it is to this day no doubt between two of the boulders.

That chance dropping of the tumbler is the archetype of those apparently inconsequential moments with Emma which had for Hardy a poetic resonance. At the time, he sketched her while she kneeled by the stream and stretched her arm down into the water. His portrayal of the scene is inscribed 'E.L.G. by T.H. Aug 19, 1870: searching for the glass (water colour sketching in Vallency valley)'. When he read her account of the incident after her death he was so moved by it that he wrote the poem 'Under the Waterfall', in which two voices – his and Emma's – recall emotions long past, culminating in Emma's conviction that the glass, 'by now with its smoothness opalized', has become a sanctified and cherished relic of their love:

> 'By night, by day, when it shines or lours,
> There lies intact that chalice of ours,
> And its presence adds to the rhyme of love

Persistently sung by the fall above.
No lip has touched it since his and mine
In turns therefrom sipped lovers' wine.'

'. . . the purl of a
little valley fall. . .'
the Vallency valley

Today the river keeps up a steady chilloping as it rushes and
tumbles over little rocky waterfalls. 'The purl of a little valley fall',
in Hardy's phrase, is the typical music of the streams of the far West

91

as they come headlong down in a steep descent from the high moors. The rivers of the Somerset Levels — the Brue and the Parrett — with their scarcely perceptible gradients are always tending to spread outwards and sideways in an obesity of water. By contrast the channels that run from the high moors to the coasts of Devon and Cornwall have the urgency of mountain streams, merry and crisp in sound and motion. The Vallency is of their company.

On either side the hills rear up, shaggy and golden with gorse. The valley is lush with a variety of deciduous trees and many flowers. Generally trees suffer in this area unless they can crouch beside some closely protecting flank of land. The mark of the gale-stormy sou'wester is sculpted on branch and trunk along the coast, stunting and bending them. The leafiness of the Vallency valley is all the more pleasing, therefore, for the relief it offers to the wind-scoured openness of the uplands. The channel of the stream is wholly enclosed overhead with interlacing branches and sprays of soft green foliage — 'arched by the oak-copse from the weather', in Hardy's words. The embowered river-bed, with its quiet pools and sparkling shallows, has a profoundly secluded and private atmosphere. Here one might reasonably expect to find shy naiads bathing, away from the vulgar pixies who infest the tourist areas.

In 1874 Emma left St Juliot to marry Hardy in a London church and spend her wedding night at Brighton. They never returned to Cornwall together. When Hardy came back to Boscastle he was in his seventies. Emma had recently died and close on forty years had passed since he last stood on Beeny, as he did now in March 1913:

> He comes and stands
> In a careworn craze,
> And looks at the sands
> And the seaward haze
> With moveless hands
> And face and gaze,
> Then turns to go . . .
> And what does he see when he gazes so?

The answer he gave to his own question was expressed in the outpouring of poems which traced again the early Cornish scenes of his courtship. Before he made this tormented pilgrimage Hardy had questioned whether the places he had once known could be said to survive any more in a recognisable sense:

> Does there even a place like Saint-Juliot exist?
> Or a Vallency Valley
> With stream and leafed alley,
> Or Beeny, or Bos with its flounce flinging mist?

He need have had no doubt. In Pentargan Bay where 'the waked birds preen and the seals flop lazily' he recaptured the sights and sounds that he and Emma had discovered together; and he could feel that, in his inner being, he was just the same as when 'Our days were a joy, and our paths through flowers'. The coastal landscapes that he drew now in verse fused together the vibrant memories of long ago with the ghost-haunted dejection of the present. In what amounted to his leave-taking of Beeny Cliff he summoned up a majestic invocation of the spirit of the place:

O the opal and the sapphire of that wandering western sea,
And the woman riding high above with bright hair flapping free –
The woman whom I loved so, and who loyally loved me.

The pale mews plained below us, and the waves seemed far away
In a nether sky, engrossed in saying their ceaseless babbling say,
As we laughed light-heartedly aloft on that clear-sunned March day.

A little cloud then cloaked us, and there flew an irised rain,
And the Atlantic dyed its levels with a dull misfeatured stain,
And then the sun burst out again, and purples prinked the main.

– Still in all its chasmal beauty bulks old Beeny to the sky,
And shall she and I not go there once again now March is nigh,
And the sweet things said in that March say anew there by and by?

What if still in chasmal beauty looms that wild weird western shore,
The woman now is – elsewhere – whom the ambling pony bore,
And nor knows nor cares for Beeny, and will laugh there nevermore.

CHAPTER SEVEN

From Plymouth to the Severn Sea

In a charmingly diffident paragraph in his preface to *A Pair of Blue Eyes*, Hardy mentioned that the setting of the story in the vicinity of 'Castle Boterel' was the furthest westward of any in which he had located what he called 'these imperfect little dramas of country life and passions'. He gives the impression that he might fittingly have refrained from crossing the Devon border, and that if he did stray a few miles beyond the Tamar he was still 'near to, or no great way beyond, the vague border of the Wessex kingdom on that side, which, like the westering verge of modern American settlements, was progressive and uncertain'. As a subject-matter this incursion into Cornwall was not a literary choice but an autobiographical necessity. His lack of any general *rapport* with the Cornish is shown in the native characters, Stephen Smith's parents, who have clearly been transported from Mellstock and bear so close a resemblance to Hardy's own parents as to be of good Dorset breed.

His only Cornish adventure away from what might be called Emma-country was in the short story 'A Mere Interlude', set mainly in Penzance – thinly disguised as Pen-Zephyr – and one of the Scilly Isles, which are named with a touch of wistfulness as the Isles of Lyonesse. Written in 1885 this is a different Lyonnesse, creating no magic in the eyes. Apart from a passing tribute to Cornish horticulture 'in this land of strawberries, these headquarters of early English flowers and fruit', the scenic background is touched in so lightly as to be featureless. The verse drama of his old age, *The Famous Tragedy of the Queen of Cornwall*, was a romantic backward look at Tintagel and 'an Iseult of my own' which bore testimony to his declining powers, and not much else. Cornwall remained a strange and legendary kingdom, in part magical and inspirational.

In lower Wessex — that is to say, in Devon — Hardy was more at ease, for this was one of his six truly Wessex counties. It borders his native Dorset, where Lambert's Castle and the downland flanking Marshwood Vale look westwards to the Axe Valley. Such towns as Axminster and Honiton would have been familiar to him. They had their counterparts in Dorset and he certainly visited Axminster in 1882, if not earlier. He paid several visits to Exeter and knew its cathedral well. In 1885 he accepted Lady Portsmouth's invitation to spend some time at Eggesford, which is situated between the Taw and Torridge rivers roughly halfway between Crediton and Barnstaple. Lord Portsmouth turned out to be 'a farmerlike man with a broad Devon accent'. He gratified Hardy's taste for the macabre by showing him a bridge 'over which bastards were thrown and drowned, even down to quite recent times'. Hardy paid a second visit in the following year. The friendship with the Portsmouths was a

Lambert's Castle Hill

strong one: Hardy noted in 1885 that Lady Portsmouth 'wants us to come to Devonshire and live near them. She says they would find a house for us. Cannot think why we live in benighted Dorset. Em would go willingly, as it is her native county; but alas, my house at Dorchester is nearly finished'.

Predictably it is Plymouth, where Emma was born, which can claim to have provided Hardy's most vivid impressions of Devonshire. The first was a happy chance: in 1873, on New Year's Eve, he bought a copy of the *Cornhill* magazine at Plymouth railway station and took it up to the Hoe where he opened it and was surprised to find that it gave pride of place to the first instalment of *Far from the Madding Crowd*. He never visited the city in Emma's company. She went alone to her father's death-bed in 1890; and a water-colour by her of Plymouth Hoe, dated 1886, suggests a previous visit. It was after her death and his reading of her childhood recollections that Hardy characteristically found an inspiration in Plymouth. Accompanied by his younger brother, Henry, he visited Plymouth in 1913 and returned there the following summer with his newly married second wife. In 1917 he and Florence were again in Plymouth but cut short their visit because of the rainy weather.

During this period Hardy was preoccupied with particular images and observations included by Emma in her memories of Plymouth as she had known it during the 1840s and 1850s. Robert Gittings has shown that several of Hardy's poems are closely linked to passages in Emma's *Some Recollections*. For example, Emma's phrase 'the streets of Plymouth, paved with marble at that time' is echoed by Hardy:

> I reach the marble-streeted town,
>   Whose 'Sound' outbreathes its air
>   Of sharp sea-salts;
> I see the movement up and down
>   As when she was there.
> Ships of all countries come and go,
>   The bandsmen boom in the sun
>   A throbbing waltz:
> The schoolgirls laugh along the Hoe
>   As when she was one.

Plymouth: the Barbican

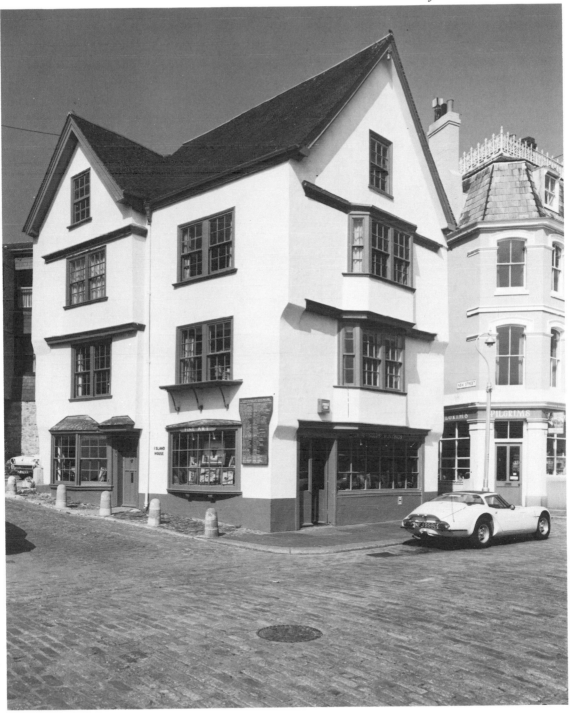

That is the first verse of the poem entitled 'The Marble-streeted Town', to which Hardy appended 'Plymouth (1914?)'. Dr Gittings points out that the 'marble' was in fact a local limestone which, particularly when wet, looked like marble. Those who recall Keats's views on the rainfall of south Devon will understand that Plymouth's streets were – more often than not – marble-like. Two other poems, 'The West-of-Wessex Girl' and 'Places', are ascribed by Hardy to Plymouth in 1913 and a third, 'Lonely Days', is acknowledged by him to be 'versified from a diary' – presumably Emma's memoir. There is a further strong presumption that one of the finest of all Hardy's poems, 'During Wind and Rain', derives from Emma's account of her early family life.

Plymouth: Sutton harbour

Plymouth Hoe

The Plymouth that he conjures up in these poems is very much a residential city, not a place of dockyards and shipping. It is a Plymouth of which few of the scenes Emma knew have survived the massive demolitions of Second World War bombing. The Plymouth of today, with its clean-cut windy streets and civic remodelling, bears a special witness to the third quarter of the twentieth century, within the age-old context of the Hoe, the Barbican and the Sound. To recapture the waterside life of Emma's Plymouth it is tempting to introduce here a neglected sketch by Wilkie Collins, from his *Rambles beyond Railways* published in 1851. On his way to a walking tour of Cornwall Collins proposed to take a boat from Plymouth past Devonport and the Tamar estuary to St Germans. Here is how his journey began:

We were lucky enough to commit ourselves, at once, to the guidance of the most amusing and original of boatmen. He was a fine, strong, swarthy fellow, with luxuriant black hair and whiskers, an irresistible broad grin, and a thoroughly good opinion of himself. He gave us his name, his autobiography, and his opinion of his own character, all in a breath. He was called William Dawle; he had begun life as a farm-labourer; then he had become a sailor in the Royal Navy, as a suitable change; now he was a licensed waterman, which was a more suitable change still; he was known all over the country; he would row against any man in England; he would take more care of us than he would of his own sons; and if we had five hundred guineas apiece in our knapsacks, he could keep no stricter watch over them than he was determined to keep now. Such was this phoenix of boatmen – under such unexceptionable auspices did we start for the shores of Cornwall.

The calm summer evening drew near its close, as we began to move through the water. The broad orb of the moon was rising dim behind us, above the dark majestic trees of Mount Edgecombe. Already, the houses of Devonport looked pale and indistinct as we left them behind us. The innumerable masts, the lofty men-of-war hulks, the drooping sails of smaller vessels – all the thickly grouped objects of the great port through which we were proceeding – assumed a solemn stillness and repose under the faint light that was now shining over them. On this wide scene, at other hours so instinct in all its parts with bustle and animation, nothing spoke now of life and action – save the lights which occasionally broke forth from houses on the hill at our side, or the small boats passing at intervals over the smooth water, and soon mysteriously lost to view behind the hull of a man-of-war, or in the deep shadows of the river's distant banks.

It was such an evening, and such a view, as I shall never forget. After enjoying the poetry and beauty of the scene uninterruptedly, for some time, we were at length recalled to practical matters of business by a species of adjuration suddenly addressed to us by that prince of British boatmen, Mr William Dawle. Resting impressively upon his oars, and assuming a deplorable expression of countenance, he respectfully requested to be informed, whether we really wished him to 'row his soul out against the tide?' – we might laugh, but would we be so kind as to step forward a minute and feel his shirt sleeves? – If we were resolved to go on, he was ready; for had he not told us that he would row against any man in England? – but he felt it due to his position as a licensed waterman, having the eyes of the public on him, and courting inspection, to inform us that 'in three parts of an hour, and no mistake,' the tide would run up; and that there was a place not far off, called Saltash – a most beautiful and interesting place, where we could get good beer. If we waited there for the turn of the tide, no race-horse that ever was foaled would take us to St Germains so fast as he would row us. In short, the point was, would we mercifully 'spare his shoulders,' or not?

As we belonged to the sauntering and vagabond order of travellers, and cared very little in how roundabout a manner we reached our destination, we inclined to the side of mercy, and spared the shoulders of Mr William Dawle; who, thereupon, reckless of the state of his shirt-sleeves, began to row again with renewed and alarming energy. Now, he bent forward over the oars, as if he was about to fall upon us – and now, he lay back from them, horizontal, and almost lost to view in the dim light. We passed, triumphantly, every boat proceeding in our direction; we brushed, at hair-breadth distances, by vessels at anchor and stakes planted in shallow water. Suddenly, what seemed to be a collection of mud hovels built upon mud, appeared in sight; shortly afterwards, our boat was grounded among a perfect legion of other boats; and the indefatigable Dawle, jumping up nimbly, seized our knapsacks and handed us out politely into the mud. We had arrived at that 'beautiful and interesting place,' Saltash.

There was no mistaking the tavern. The only light on shore gleamed from the tavern window; and, judging by the criterion of noise, the whole local population seemed to be collected within the tavern walls. We opened the door; and found ourselves in a small room, filled with shrimpers, sailors, fishermen and watermen, all 'looming large' through a fog of tobacco, and all chirping merrily over their cups; while the hostess sat apart on a raised seat in a corner, calm and superior amidst the hubbub, as Neptune himself, when he rose to the surface to save the pious Eneas from shipwreck, at the crisis of the storm. As there was no room for us in this festive hall, we were indulged in the luxury of a private apartment, where Mr Dawle proceeded to 'do the honours' of Saltash, by admonishing

101

the servant to be particular about the quality of the ale she brought, dusting chairs with the crown of his hat, proposing toasts and sentiments, snuffing the candle briskly with his fingers, and other pleasant social attentions of a similar nature. Having, as he imagined, sufficiently propitiated us by this course of conduct, he started an entirely new proposition – which bore reference, however, to the old subject of mercifully sparing his shoulders, and was expressed to the following effect: – Might he go now, and fetch his 'missus,' who lived hard by? She was the very nicest and strongest woman in Saltash; was able to row almost as well as he could, and would help him materially in getting to St Germains; but perhaps we objected to admit her into the boat? We had but to say the word, if we did; and from that moment forth, he was dumb on the subject for ever.

How could we resist this most irresistible of boatmen? There was something about his inveterate good-humour and inveterate idleness, his comical variations backwards and forwards between great familiarity and great respect, his honesty on one point (he asked us no more than his proper fare in the first instance) and his manoeuvring on another, that would have cajoled a Cynic into complacency. Besides, our innate sentiments of gallantry forbade the thought of objecting to the company and assistance of Mrs William Dawle! So, we sent the fortunate spouse of this strong and useful woman, to seek her forthwith – and forthwith did he return, with a very remarkable species of 'missus,' in the shape of a gigantic individual of the male sex – the stoutest, strongest, and the hairiest man I ever saw – who entered, exhaling a relishing odour of shrimps, with his shirt-sleeves rolled up to his shoulders! 'Gentlemen both, good evening,' said this urbane giant, looking dreamily forward two feet over our heads, and then settling himself solemnly on a bench – never more to open his lips in our presence!

Our worthy boatman's explanation of the phenomenon he had thus presented to us, involved some humiliating circumstances. His 'missus' had flatly refused to aid her lord and master in the exertion of rowing, and had practically carried out her refusal by immediately going to bed before his face. As for the shrimp-flavoured giant, Mr Dawle informed me (in a whisper) that his name was 'Dick;' that he had met him outside, and had asked him to favour us with his company, because he was a very amusing man, if we could only bring him out; and was capable of beguiling the time, while we were waiting for the tide, by an excellent story or two. Presuming that a fresh supply of ale was all that was wanting to develop the latent humour of our new friend, we ordered a second quart; but it unhappily produced no effect. (It would have required, I am inclined to think, a gallon to have attained the desired result.) 'Dick' sat voiceless and vacant, staring steadily at the candle, and occasionally groaning softly to himself, as if he had something dreadful on his mind and dared not disburthen it in company.

There were further humorous adventures before St Germans was reached but it is sufficiently clear already that William Dawle would be entirely at home with the Mellstock Quire in *Under the Greenwood Tree* and comfortably at ease with the company at the Old Maltster's in *Far from the Madding Crowd*. Hardy's senior contemporary was not only a model for the melodrama of *Desperate Remedies*: he was fully proficient in the satirically quaint caricaturing of rustic and provincial working-men, at which Hardy excelled subsequently.

The pity is that Hardy's skill in prose-fiction found no real opportunity in Devon. Although it was in his day the second largest English county – only Yorkshire surpassing it – he made little impression on it, or it on him. In the north of the county he set one short story, 'The Honourable Laura'; he set a second, 'The Romantic Adventures of a Milkmaid', in the south. Neither is of much substance. 'The Honourable Laura' contains glimpses of Woody Bay and Coombe Martin (alias 'Cliff-Martin') but only to provide a cliff for pushing someone over. 'The Romantic Adventures of a Milkmaid' is set in the Exe Valley, at Silverton, and Sidmouth is also involved; but Hardy wrote the story hurriedly at Wimborne in the winter of 1882/83 with the familiar background of the Frome valley originally in his mind, and only later transposed it to Devonshire, needing perhaps to keep this minor milkmaid quite separate from Tess. The one touch of Devonian verisimilitude he added, beyond the changing of place-names, was the fluted 'u' sound which is so instantly typical of the county's vernacular accent.

The thinness of Devon material in Hardy's writings prompts certain speculations that are worth pursuing. The first concerns his mobility before and during the years when he was writing novels. According to Michael Millgate it was 1896 when Hardy first rode

103

a bicycle. In his later years he made increasing use of a motor-car to travel around Wessex. Before 1896, however, he had to rely on the railway for longer distances, and on walking or some kind of horse-drawn vehicle for lesser journeys. He knew Dorset thoroughly, not only from the stronghold of his native home but also from lodgings in Weymouth and the centres of his married residence at Dorchester, Swanage, Wimborne and Sturminster Newton. His opportunities to explore the wider field of Wessex in his formative years were more limited than might at first appear. He had neither the time nor the transport for detailed, extensive explorations. One of the solutions to the problem was for him to conceive characters, dialogue and landscape in his native Dorset terms and then to transpose the finished work by the literary equivalent of an actor's make-up — an alteration of place-names, a change of dialect, an emphasis on a well-known landmark. 'The Romantic Adventures of a Milk-maid' is an example of just such a method.

There is another factor which may be peculiar to Devon. In the north of the county, and extending into Somerset, a rival 'kingdom' was already established — the Lorna Doone country of R. D. Blackmore. In some ways it was a model for Hardy to follow elsewhere, not to compete with on its own ground. Just as I have been inside the cottage where Tess was 'born', so equally I have held Jan Ridd's 'girt, big gun' — or supposedly so. With its traditional love of legends the West Country regards its cherished fictions as embodiments of truths more impregnable than any mere facts.

Hardy's relationship in his early years as a novelist with Blackmore is revealing. *Lorna Doone* was first published in 1869 but Hardy did not read it until after he had published *Far from the Madding Crowd*. Writing in 1875 to Blackmore, who was fifteen years older than himself, Hardy said:

> I have just read your finest book (as I think) — Lorna Doone, and I cannot help writing just one line to tell you how astonished I was to find what it contained — exquisite ways of describing things which are more after my own heart than the 'presentations' of any other writer that I am acquainted with ... Little phases of nature which I thought nobody had noticed but myself were continually turning up in your book ... A kindred sentiment between us in so many things is, I suppose, partly because we both spring from the West of England.

This tribute to Blackmore recognises that, like William Barnes, he was a pioneer in the creation of a 'West of England' consciousness. *Lorna Doone* is probably too sweet for today's palate, particularly in the idealisation of its heroine, but it remains a powerful landmark in the evolution of 'Wessex'. Jan Ridd has obvious affinities with Gabriel Oak and Giles Winterborne in his modestly self-conscious pride as a Westcountryman. These were new hero-figures, with their strong regional overtones. The affectionately detailed presentation of landscape and speech, emphasising the specifically local flavour and vernacular style, is another close link between Blackmore and Hardy: so is the slyly humorous sense of class distinctions in Jan's description of his mother as 'being of good draper family, and polished above the yeomanry'.

For a winter's landscape to set beside Tess's Flintcomb-Ash, Blackmore can offer this:

> Now a strange thing came to pass that winter, when I was twenty-one years old, a very strange thing, which affrighted the rest and made me feel uncomfortable. Not that there was anything in it, to do harm to any one, only that none could explain it, except by attributing it to the devil. The weather was very mild and open, and scarcely any snow fell; at any rate none lay on the ground even for an hour, in the highest part of Exmoor; a thing which I knew not before nor since, as long as I can remember. But the nights were wonderfully dark, as though with no stars in the heaven; and all day long the mists were rolling upon the hills and down them, as if the whole land were a wash-house. The moorland was full of snipes and teal, and curlews flying and crying, and lapwings flapping heavily, and ravens hovering round dead sheep; yet no redshanks nor dottrell, and scarce any golden plovers (of which we have great store generally) but vast lonely birds, that cried at night, and moved the whole air with their pinions; yet no man ever saw them.

When he came to the representation of dialect speech Blackmore shared Barnes's desire to set down not only the vocabulary and structure but the precise sound, as nearly as he could do so by variations of spelling. When John Fry is handling the gun of the late Jan Ridd senior, who was unarmed when the Doones murdered him, he comments:

'Bad job for he, as her had not got thiccy, the naight as her coom acrass them Doones. Rackon Varmer Jan 'ood a-zhown them the wai to Kingdom come, 'stead of going herzell zo aisy. And a maight have been gooin' to market now, 'stead of laying banked up, over yanner'.

'Thic' or 'thiccy' was widely current in Wessex and is still heard as a dialect form of 'this' or 'this here'. Particularly interesting is 'her' which in the context is not feminine. It is the male pronoun, a form of the Teutonic 'er', easy to sound but difficult to write. Shakespeare renders it as 'a': in *Much Ado*, for example, 'If he be not in love with some woman, there is no believing old signs: a' brushes his hat o' mornings'. Blackmore tries it as an alternative to 'her' in 'a maight have been gooin' to market'. Hardy, always sparing of such devices, nevertheless follows Shakespeare in this one: 'a' for 'he' occurs frequently in his dialogue. In *The Woodlanders* he went one further, suggesting Grammer Oliver's old-fashioned way of talking by her use of 'Ich' for 'I'. The Saxon influence is tenacious and enduring, particularly in Somerset and Dorset, where the aspirated 'r' at the beginning of a word may still be heard – 'rain' being pronounced as 'hrain'.

The Exmoor of *Lorna Doone* was already losing its primitive nature in the lifetime of Blackmore and Hardy, with the new enclosures of land and the investment of capital by a Midlands ironmaster intent on modernising its way of life. Even so, in comparison with Dartmoor it has been spared some of the more familiar pressures of modern times. Dartmoor has to cope with the presence of the Army and the proximity of the big urban concentrations of Plymouth and Torbay. It opposes and must be reconciled with the main westward drive of traffic from Exeter.

Exmoor is not on the way to anywhere more important than Barnstaple and Bideford. North Devon in general remains lightly populated – even sparsely so in places. The honeymoon coast so popular with the later Victorian and Edwardian couples, who returned to the surburbs of cities to settle in bijou villas named *Lynmouth* and *Ilfracombe*, retains its modest scale. Although it lacks the severity of Dartmoor's granite tors, Exmoor's softer landscape is far from being tame. The buzzard and the red deer are its familiars; the siege by snow is its commonplace winter hazard.

Granted that he lacked the close experience to handle it in the prose detail of a story, Hardy responded in his poetry to Exmoor and to its neighbouring Somerset areas of the Quantocks and Taunton Dene. The peaks of Dunkery Beacon and Wills Neck provide the characteristic symbols that he uses so readily to call up a landscape. In *Wessex Heights* the range of hill-tops on which he meditates extends from Inkpen Beacon, the point where the Hampshire Downs merge into the Wiltshire-Berkshire borderland, to the Quantocks vantage-point commanding the Bristol Channel coast, in a single ringing line – 'Say, on Ingpen Beacon eastward, or on Wylls-Neck westwardly'.

A similar but more elaborate highlighting is given to Exmoor and Dunkery Beacon in the narrative poem 'The Sacrilege'. Described by Hardy as a 'ballad-tragedy' this powerful story in verse of jealousy and murder ranges over Somerset in a way that rivals an even finer ballad with a Somerset setting, 'The Trampwoman's Tragedy'. Both poems follow the fortunes of disreputable wanderers in the rural underworld of gipsies, petty thieves and vagabonds.

Exmoor: northern approach to Dunkery Beacon

'While Dunkery frowns on Exon Moor'

'The Sacrilege' describes an act of theft in Wells Cathedral by a travelling man who lives in a van on Exmoor – 'on Exon Wild by Dunkery Tor'. To please the fickle woman who lives with him he has previously stolen 'a silken kerchief crimson-red' off a market stall in the Mendip village of Priddy. His rival for this woman's love is 'the Cornish Wrestler Joe' whom she threatens to meet for 'dance and dallyings'. Cornish wrestling, I should mention in passing, is a specialised form of combat which the Cornish share with the Bretons: tournaments between the two peoples have been a historic link across the English Channel. Hardy's choice of this character as the gipsy's rival is an instance of his quick, sure touch in the evocation of Wessex life.

The price the gipsy must pay for the woman's constancy is to raid Wells Cathedral, as he recounts to his twin brother whom he charges to avenge him if the plot fails:

'And as she drowsed within my van
On Exon Wild by Dunkery Tor –
And as she drowsed within my van,
    And dawning turned to day,
She heavily raised her sloe-black eyes
And murmured back in softest wise,
"One more thing, and the charms you prize
    Are yours henceforth for aye.

'"And swear I will I'll never go
While Dunkery frowns on Exon Moor
To meet the Cornish Wrestler Joe
    For dance and dallyings.
If you'll to yon cathedral shrine,
And finger from the chest divine
Treasure to buy me ear-drops fine,
    And richly jewelled rings."

'I said: "I am one who has gathered gear
From Marlbury Downs to Dunkery Tor,
Who has gathered gear for many a year
    From mansion, mart and fair;
But at God's house I've stayed my hand,
Hearing within me some command –
Curbed by a law not of the land
    From doing damage there!"

He is persuaded, however, to commit the act of sacrilege, is caught redhanded and subsequently hanged 'in Toneborough Town by Exon Moor'. When his mistress takes up again with the Cornish wrestler she is murdered by the gipsy's brother.

For Hardy the ballad narrative is one of the most effective ways of sketching his impressions of Wessex scenes and characters. In the movement of his verse-stories he can make good use of a momentary glimpse of some town or hill or noteworthy landmark. To leave Somerset momentarily, the journey from London to Exeter in the poem 'My Cicely' is a good example of this infused interest in what is otherwise a second-rate piece. Following the classic westward route, in the eighteenth century, over Bagshot Heath he recalls the gallant defence of Basing House as he passes through Basingstoke to

109

Salisbury, where the cathedral brings to mind the name of its foun-
der, Richard Poore. After a change of horses the rider takes the
Great Western Turnpike across Cranborne Chase to Blandford
Forum, traversing Oakley Down where the Roman road runs along-
side 'the bleak hill-graves of Chieftains'. And so onward to the
familiar landmarks of Hardy's native landscapes, Weatherbury
Castle (*alias* Weatherby Castle, south of Milborne St Andrew),
Casterbridge itself, Maiden Castle and Eggardon; and the final stage:

> The Nine-Pillared Cromlech, the Bride-streams,
> The Axe and the Otter
> I passed, to the gate of the city
> Where Exe scents the sea.

The Nine-Pillared Cromlech is the 'miniature Stonehenge', in J.O.
Bailey's description, known as Nine Stones at Winterborne Abbas.
It is perhaps significant that it is the last precise landmark mentioned by Hardy; as his itinerary passes into less familiar country
he contents himself with mentioning the rivers a rider would cross.
The Bride-streams are the river Bride and its tributaries, flowing
through Long Bredy to Burton Bradstock.

Hardy's own view of this poem as a useful way of conveying his
broad sense of the Wessex countryside was given in a letter he
wrote in 1908 to Harry Pouncy, a Dorchester journalist who gave
lectures on Hardy's writings – 'By the way, if you wanted more
views, or rather new things to say, the poem "My Cicely" in the
Wessex Poems would afford a capital panoramic treatment of the
Great Western Road from London to Exeter – accompanied by your
recitation of the journey with the galloping movement of the
verses'.

The poem brings a vivacity to the itinerary but Hardy does not
always escape the traps that await the unwary in taking a hint from
a name. Blandford Forum certainly invites the embroidery 'Along
through the Stour-bordered Forum/Where Legions had wayfared,'
but Blandford (*alias* 'Shottsford') was not a Roman town. The
Roman road from Badbury Rings to Dorchester crossed the Stour at
Shapwick, about halfway between Blandford and Wimborne.

Hardy is on surer ground in 'Molly Gone', where he recalls the
outings he shared with his sister Mary: particularly north of
Beaminster to Whitesheet Hill and Winyards Gap, a favourite view-

point across the Somerset border 'catching Montacute Crest/To the right against Sedgemoor, and Corton-Hill's far distant cap'.

Montacute, for long the home of the Phelips family, now belongs to the National Trust. Corton Hill is a few miles north of Sherborne. This area of south Somerset is a part of Wessex that Hardy knew well. His sole place of residence in Wessex outside Dorset was here, at Yeovil, though admittedly for only a few months in 1876. He explored the surrounding countryside, in May visiting Closworth, where he noticed a curious luminous effect in some cowslips in an orchard – 'A light proceeds from them, as from Chinese lanterns or glow-worms'. It is tempting to see in this the genesis of the famous scene of gambling by the light of glow-worms in the novel he started shortly afterwards, *The Return of the Native*.

The contrast between north Dorset and south Somerset is particularly marked in the vicinity of Winyards Gap. On the Dorset side the downland heights slope southward and the rivers that rise *Montacute House*

within the county flow to the English Channel. The Somerset rivers flow northwards from the watershed, winding sluggishly across the low moors to Bridgwater Bay and the Severn Sea, as the Bristol Channel is sometimes named. With the change of aspect goes a profound geological change: the chalk and limestone of Dorset give way to the blue lias clay of the Somerset Levels.

The source of the river Parrett is almost within sight of Winyards Gap. Its first stage is through the foothills that form the semicircle of higher land enclosing Sedgemoor and the Vale of Avalon – a semicircle ranging from the Mendips to the Blackdown Hills and the Quantocks. It is along the central sector of this semicircle that the Fosse Way runs, emphasising the changing character of the Somerset landscape. Between the Fosse Way and Bridgwater Bay the low moors were barely habitable and often impassable. The Roman villas that flourished along the Fosse Way in central Somerset were on the edge of a civilisation.

Despite its proximity Somerset did not provide Hardy with a major landscape in prose. His novels and short stories do not point to anything comparable with the north coast of Cornwall or Egdon Heath: it is in his poetry that the county is rendered most memorably. 'Stancy Castle' in one of his less successful novels, *A Laodicean*, is evidently intended by Hardy to be identified in some degree with Dunster Castle, but its details are drawn from other sources. Re-reading the novel thirty years later he commented, in the 1912 preface, that 'its sites, mileages and architectural details can hardly seem satisfactory to the investigating topographist, so appreciable a proportion of these features being but the baseless fabrics of a vision'. The echo of Prospero's words in *The Tempest* is a graceful reminder of the freedom with which Hardy adapts, and sometimes departs from, a literal transcript of the 'real' world.

The short story, 'A Tragedy of Two Ambitions', is set in the Coker villages without evoking any sense of place. The story for children, 'Our Exploits at West Poley', similarly makes only a perfunctory use of its Mendip setting: Wookey suggests itself as the original of the cave but the villages of East and West Poley remain obstinately fictitious. Bath makes several incidental appearances in Hardy's fiction but the spirits that haunt its squares and crescents and assembly-rooms are Sheridan's and Jane Austen's rather than Hardy's.

For a truer vision of Somerset we must look northward from Winyards Gap with the poet's eye. There is first the lushness of the scene, with the sweet tall grass brushing the teats of the cows, and the abundance of apple-blossom. In 'The Dance at the Phoenix' the rural lover from Somerset has a freshness and innocence which set him apart from the soldiers of the King's Own Cavalry:

Mendip: looking towards Wookey from Ebbor Gorge

> To Jenny came a gentle youth
> From inland leazes lone,
> His love was fresh as apple-blooth
> By Parrett, Yeo, or Tone.

In 'Growth in May' Hardy revels in the sheer copiousness of Nature near Chard as he knew it when he was living at Yeovil:

113

I enter a daisy-and-buttercup land,
    And thence thread a jungle of grass:
Hurdles and stiles scarce visible stand
    Above the lush stems as I pass.

Hedges peer over, and try to be seen,
    And seem to reveal a dim sense
That amid such ambitious and elbow-high green
    They make a mean show as a fence.

Further into Somerset the scene and the mood change. Ham Hill and Montacute Crest stand out in isolation as the lie of the land begins to fall away to the low moors. From Ham Hill comes the most beautiful of building-stones that Sylvia Townsend Warner described as 'honey-coloured', and Hardy as 'snuff-coloured'. Its warmth of tone is a constant delight in so many of the churches and manor-houses of central Wessex. Appropriately, at the end of his

View from Ham Hill towards Norton sub Hamdon

life it was 'by his wish' that the car conveying Hardy home from
Ilminster was driven past the quarries where Ham Hill stone was
cut, in what may fairly be interpreted as a final salute from a poet
who was also an architect.

From Stoke-under-Ham, where even the *pissoir* of a pub is of the
local stone, to Somerton is barely seven miles as the crow flies; but
the buildings of Somerton are, by contrast, as good an example as
may be found of the blue lias stone. It is the blue lias that dominates
the moors to the coastal strip of brick-clay which gave Bridgwater
its brick and tile industry. These transitions are reflected in landscape and atmosphere, which lend themselves to darker moods of
melancholy and superstition. The poem 'Vagg Hollow' takes us into
the area of Ilchester and Tintinhull and the Victorian canal system
that for a time gave Langport an importance for waterborne traffic.
The poem describes the response of a waggoner's lad to a haunted
spot on the road, which was the subject of a superstition that Hardy
noted in April, 1902:

> Vagg Hollow, on the way to Load Bridge (Somerset) is a place
> where 'things' used to be seen – usually taking the form of a wool-
> pack in the middle of the road. Teams and other horses always
> stopped on the brow of the hollow, and could only be made to
> go on by whipping. A waggoner once cut at the pack with his
> whip: it opened in two, and smoke and a hoofed figure rose out
> of it.

It seems likely that Hardy picked up this strange story during a
bicycle ride he made at that time across 'sad Sedgemoor' to the
Polden Hills and Glastonbury. In a letter to Edmund Gosse describing the ride he revealed that it also gave him the inspiration for what
he considered to be 'upon the whole, his most successful poem' –
'A Trampwoman's Tragedy'.

The word *Sedgemoor* reverberates with the awesome sound of a
muffled bell in the depths of Wessex memories. It calls up the
hopelessness of the Duke of Monmouth's Rebellion; the last battle
fought on English soil, on the moor near Westonzoyland; and the
merciless aftermath of the Bloody Assizes, when men were hanged
naked and in chains. In Ilchester gaol the Quaker, John Whiting,
witnessed the execution of eight men who were quartered and their
bowels burnt in front of the prison windows, to the shame of those

115

*King's Sedgemoor
Drain*

he condemned for 'forcing poor men to hale about men's quarters, like horse-flesh or carrion, to boil and hang them up as monuments.'

Like many another Westcountryman Hardy had his own family memories of the Rebellion. One of his mother's ancestors was accused of being absent from home at the time – the presumption being that he was therefore with the rebels – and Hardy suggests that, if he escaped execution, he was probably transported. Another family tradition provided the basis for the short story 'The Duke's Reappearance'.

The tale that occupied his thoughts during his bicycle ride in the spring of 1902 was not a family one, however, but concerned a woman named Mary Ann Taylor who was involved in a tragic incident in 1827 – the details of which Hardy claimed to have known 'for many years'. She was a trampwoman who wandered with her 'fancy-man' over much of Wessex including the New Forest, Marshwood Vale, and most of Somerset from Mendip to the western moors. Travelling with them were another couple, 'jeering' John and Mother Lee. To tease her lover Mary pretended to flirt with John, but the joke misfired and John was murdered in a fit of jealousy. It is at Winyard's Gap that Hardy opens the story:

From Wynyard's Gap the livelong day,
    The livelong day,
We beat afoot the northward way
    We had travelled times before.
The sun-blaze burning on our backs,
Our shoulders sticking to our packs,
By fosseway, fields, and turnpike tracks
    We skirted sad Sedge-Moor.

Full twenty miles we jaunted on,
    We jaunted on, –
My fancy-man, and jeering John,
    And Mother Lee, and I.
And, as the sun drew down to west,
We climbed the toilsome Polden crest,
And saw, of landskip sights the best,
    The inn that beamed thereby.

Greylake: looking
south-east over
King's Sedgemoor

The Polden Hills are a remarkable feature of central Somerset. Although they never rise above a modest 300 feet or thereabouts, they rear up so sharply and positively from the flat land on either side that they take on an exalted presence out of all proportion to their size. No major road crosses them. Along their length they support the historic link between the neighbourhood of Glastonbury and the outer settlements of Bridgwater. They make a clearly defined frontier between the pastures and withy beds of the Sedgemoor side and what William Stradling called 'the immense turbary' – that strange landscape of peat workings in what used to be Brent Marsh before the Ordnance Survey, on a romantic impulse, renamed it 'the Vale of Avalon'.

There are more ways than one of going from Winyard's Gap to the inn on the Poldens where jeering John was murdered. Through Ilchester and Somerton would be one way: another would be to follow the course of the Parrett to the vicinity of Muchelney Abbey where the river recruits its two important tributaries, the Isle and the Yeo, and thence through Langport. The first comes more directly to 'Polden Crest' and the inn 'far-famed as "Marshal's Elm" '; the second lies nearer to the battlefield of 'sad Sedgemoor' and would follow the Greylake Fosse across King's Sedgemoor Drain to the Poldens at Greinton.

It was at Ilchester, in the notoriously fever-ridden and now vanished jail, that John's killer was hanged. Outside the jail the trampwoman gave birth to her fancy-man's child, with none to help her since Mother Lee had died at Glastonbury. The setting of the story may be fortuitous but there is no doubt that the names Hardy uses in this tragedy – 'sad Sedgemoor, Ivel-chester jail, Glaston, the western moors' – touch deep chords in the folk-memory of Wessex.

'Marshal's Elm' ceased to be an inn before the end of the last century and became a farmhouse, enjoying today a different fame for the prize-winning livestock bred on the farm. The name derives from John Marshall who died about 1467 and held the manor of Ivethorn of the abbot of Glastonbury: the Ivythorn land along the crest, beautifully wooded and commanding a fine view of Sedgemoor, now belongs to the National Trust. In its earlier history the inn was the scene of another violent death. One of the first skirmishes of the Civil War took place here when the Royalists are said to have sustained their first fatal casualty.

The positioning of the inn makes this one of the most arresting look-out points in the county, indeed in Wessex. To stand here is to comprehend in full measure the trampwoman's words:

'Sad Sedgemoor'
from Walton Hill

> Beneath us figured tor and lea,
> From Mendip to the western sea —
> I doubt if finer sight there be
> Within this royal realm.

Looking to the south-west from the Ivythorn side the eye ranges over Sedgemoor to Othery and Burrow Mump and King Alfred's fastness at Athelney in his darkest hour; northwards from the But-leigh side of the old inn it is the conical tor of Glastonbury, with the ruined chapel of St Michael on its summit, which at once seizes

119

attention. As you look down on the softly yielding, fen-like moors the emblematic presence of Glastonbury seems to reverberate like a gong in the surrounding silence. Nowhere in Wessex conjures up so striking a continuity of our history as here – from the Stone Age men and animals of the Mendip caves to the track-ways and axes of the Bronze Age preserved in the peat of Brent Marsh; and so to the Glastonbury Bowl and the many other surviving evidences of the Lake Villages at Meare and Godney where the last generations of prehistory saw the arrival of the Romans, and the misty legends of Glastonbury began to swirl about the Isle of Avalon. Demonstrable facts and the plausibilities of 'tradition' seem inextricable here, so that one wonders what transpositions of reality are needed to bring King Alfred and King Arthur on to the same plane of 'truth' – Alfred, 'England's Darling', building at Athelney his vanished abbey of thanksgiving; Arthur supposedly buried in the great abbey of Glastonbury, between the ruined arches that still grope upwards like blinded giants. It was instinctively the man of Wessex who in 1914 wrote the poem 'Channel Firing', in which the sound of the guns is heard:

> As far inland as Stourton Tower,
> And Camelot, and starlit Stonehenge.

The three places bring together Alfred, Arthur and the nameless hero-kings of prehistory. Stourton Tower, also known as the Alfred Tower, was erected in his honour in 1766 near Stourhead and is a familiar landmark there. Camelot has been identified as Cadbury Castle, which adjoins the valley of the Cam and the Camel villages, to the south-east of Glastonbury.

Hardy visited Glastonbury on at least three occasions. In 1902 it was the destination of the cycle ride during which he composed the trampwoman poem. Two years later he cycled there again and spent 'a romantic day or two among the ruins'. In 1924 he returned to witness his verse-play, *The Queen of Cornwall*, in the musical version that Rutland Boughton had created as part of his Glastonbury Festival, where *The Immortal Hour* also had its first production.

The nearby hills of Mendip have a further interest than their presence in 'Our Exploits at West Poley'. In addition to the lead the Romans mined, they contain reddle – the red ochre that Diggory Venn hawked over Egdon Heath. From the quarry at Winford the

'Beneath us figured tor and lea'

travelling reddleman would have carried his cargo to shepherds who wanted the red powder for their sheep, to cheesemakers who coloured the outer linen on their ripening cheeses with it, and also perhaps to a proud housewife who liked to smarten her front doorstep with it. Nowadays it is mainly used as an ingredient in paint.

Bath occasioned a couple of indifferent poems but it is as a subject for comic prose that it drew from Hardy a virtuoso passage of dialogue. In *Far from the Madding Crowd* Cainy Ball returns from a visit to Bath and is questioned by the harvest workers about the sights he saw, to which he replies:

> 'Great glass windows to the shops, and great clouds in the sky, full of rain, and old wooden trees in the country round.'
> 'You stun-poll! What will ye say next?' said Coggan.
> 'Let en alone,' interposed Joseph Poorgrass. 'The boy's maning is that the sky and the earth in the kingdom of Bath is not altogether different from ours here. 'Tis for our good to gain knowledge of strange cities, and as such the boy's words should be suffered, so to speak it.'

'And the people of Bath,' continued Cain, 'never need to light their fires except as a luxury, for the water springs up out of the earth ready boiled for use.'

''Tis true as the light,' testified Matthew Moon, 'I've heard other navigators say the same thing.'

'They drink nothing else there,' said Cain, 'and seem to enjoy it, to see how they swaller it down.'

'Well, it seems a barbarian practice enough to us, but I daresay the natives think nothing o' it,' said Matthew.

'And don't victuals spring up as well as drink?' asked Coggan, twirling his eye.

'No – I own to a blot there in Bath – a true blot. God didn't provide 'em with victuals as well as drink, and 'twas a drawback I couldn't get over at all.'

'Well, 'tis a curious place, to say the least,' observed Moon; 'and it must be a curious people that live therein.'

The coast of Somerset towards Minehead

CHAPTER EIGHT

The Channel Coast

The English Channel coast of Hardy's Wessex extends effectively from Southampton Water to Plymouth Sound. In Cornwall it was the northern Atlantic coast that mattered. In Hampshire Portsmouth was neglected by Hardy: H.M.S. *Victory* was still afloat in *The Dynasts* and *The Trumpet-Major*. Southsea ('Solentsea') provided the setting for the short story 'An Imaginative Woman' but it displayed little more than a terrace-house on the sea front with 'a small garden of wind-proof and salt-proof evergreens'. On holiday here, Ella Marchmill passed the time in bathing or listening to the Green Silesian band while her husband went sailing.

In the whole body of Hardy's writing the imagery of the countryside is so powerful that it is easy to overlook the fact that the sea was always a near neighbour. Dorchester, as he pointed out, was 'near enough to the sea to get very distinct whiffs of marine air'. From his birthplace to Weymouth is no more than ten miles and he certainly visited the town in his boyhood, accompanying his father on one occasion 'as a treat', when Mr Hardy drove to Weymouth to attend to some business there.

The importance of the sea-coast to Wessex people can hardly be exaggerated. One has only to imagine a defensive arc from Gloucester to Southampton – no great distance – to complete the insular nature of the south-west peninsula as a separate kingdom. For the people of Wessex the sea has been historically their living, their adventure and their peril. I recall an old Brixham fisherman saying proudly, 'The history of England is written on the gravestones of the West Country fishing-villages' – which may not be the whole truth but is a decent part of it. To go to sea from a Devon farm or a Dorset village was no great step and no surprise.

The dual nature of the Channel coast is made very clear by Hardy. *Weymouth harbour*
It is firstly an invasion coast, a line of defence, an ultimate frontier:
on the inside is home and security, on the outside is 'foreignness'
and danger. Hardy's elders had lived through one of the most
intense periods of invasion fear and his childhood impressions were
coloured by their reminiscences. On the other side of the coin, the
Channel coast is the outward gateway for crusaders, adventurers,
troopships, tourists and miscellaneous visitors to 'the Continent',
the European mainland, or even more distant goals.

Southampton is an appropriate starting-point. It was up
Southampton water that the vanguard of the invading Saxons came
in 495 to found eventually the kingdom of Wessex. And it was here
in 1899 that Hardy watched the embarcation of troops for the Boer
War:

125

Here, where Vespasian's legions struck the sands,
And Cerdic with his Saxons entered in,
And Henry's army leapt afloat to win
Convincing triumphs over neighbour lands,

Vaster battalions press for further strands,
To argue in the selfsame bloody mode
Which this late age of thought, and pact, and code,
Still fails to mend.

Hardy wrote three poems describing the incidents of that October
day at Southampton docks and more followed during the course of
the war, including one of his greatest – the strange visionary piece
entitled 'The Souls of the Slain'. In it he imagines himself alone at
night on Portland Bill looking out over the turbulent currents of the
'Race', while the souls of men killed in Africa are homing overhead:

Soon from out of the Southward seemed nearing
A whirr, as of wings
Waved by mighty-vanned flies,
Or by night-moths of measureless size,
And in softness and smoothness well-nigh beyond hearing
Of corporal things.

Their motive in returning is 'to feast on our fame', but it is not their
'glory and war-mightiness' that their kindred value, but the ordinary things of the domestic life from which they sailed away. For
some there would be an affectionate homecoming, for others not.

Thus speaking, the trooped apparitions
Began to disband
And resolve them in two:
Those whose record was lovely and true
Bore to northward for home: those of bitter traditions
Again left the land,

And, towering to seaward in legions,
They paused at a spot
Overbending the Race –
That engulphing, ghast, sinister place –
Whither headlong they plunged, to the fathomless regions
Of myriads forgot.

The Boer War and the Great War of 1914–18 were the two wars that Hardy lived through but it was a third war – the Napoleonic – that most deeply and enduringly preoccupied him. The coastal area surrounding Weymouth Bay was eloquent with memories of the local volunteers training to defend their homes, of the signal-beacons primed ready to give the alarm, of the King himself at Weymouth inspecting his troops and being cheered by sailors who – as Fanny Burney noted – would start to huzza if they saw no more than the regal shadow.

The Trumpet-Major and *The Dynasts* are the principal fruits of Hardy's lifelong interest in the subject. When he completed *The Dynasts* Hardy remarked, in a letter to his friend, Edward Clodd, 'I have been living in Wellington's campaigns so much lately that, like George IV, I am almost positive that I took part in the battle of Waterloo, and have written of it from memory'. In addition to these major works Hardy returned again and again to some 'memory' of

Chalk figure of George III near Osmington

those wartime years in his poems and stories. The popular beauty-spot at Lulworth Cove, for instance, is the scene of Solomon Selby's story, 'A Tradition of 1804'. Solomon was a shepherd's son who took his turn at tending the lambing-ewes by night on the downs above the Cove. His story began on

> . . . one of those very still nights when, if you stand on the high hills anywhere within two or three miles of the sea, you can hear the rise and fall of the tide along the shore, coming and going every few moments like a sort of great snore of the sleeping world.

While the world slept Solomon saw two men enter the Cove, French generals, holding and examining a chart; and he realised that one of the men was Bonaparte himself – 'the Corsican ogre' – choosing a location for the landing of his invasion-force. Hardy later admitted that this 'tradition' was a fabrication of his own: even so it is as compelling as many a legend of more respectably anonymous origins.

Lulworth Cove

A tradition closer to truth is embodied in the poem 'The Alarm', where the central figure – the Volunteer – is based on Hardy's grandfather. The Local Volunteers served the same purpose as the 1940 Home Guard, who incidentally were known first as Local Defence Volunteers. Hardy treated his grandfather's military service in the 'Green Linnets' with proper respect but he made a figure of fun of that other Volunteer, Grandfer Cantle in *The Return of the Native*.

> 'Why, afore I went a soldier in the Bang-up Locals (as we was called), in the year four,' chimed in Grandfer Cantle brightly, 'I didn't know no more what the world was like than the commonest man among ye. And now, jown it all, I won't say what I bain't fit for, hey?'

> 'In the year four 'twas said there wasn't a finer figure in the whole South Wessex than I, as I looked when dashing past the shop-winders with the rest of our company on the day we ran out o'Budmouth because it was thought that Boney had landed round the point. There was I, straight as a young poplar, wi' my firelock, and my bagnet, and my spatterdashes, and my stock sawing my jaws off, and my accoutrements sheening like the seven stars! Yes, neighbours, I was a pretty sight in my soldiering days.'

'Bang-up' was slang of the period, equivalent to slap-up or smart: in 1818 the *Sherborne Mercury* referred to 'The Bang-up Post-coach'.

We catch another glimpse of Private Cantle in *The Dynasts*, in the scene on Rainbarrow when the beacon is lit in the course of a false alarm. The lighting of warning fires on the hill-tops behind the Channel was a traditional signal: during the threat of Napoleonic invasion bonfires were maintained in readiness at many points. Into his research notes for *The Trumpet-Major* Hardy copied a letter of 12 October 1803 from the Lord Lieutenant of Dorset (the Earl of Dorchester) to Henry Bankes of Kingston Lacy, whose estate there included Badbury Rings, in respect of which these instructions were given:

> I have to beg of you that you will give directions for an assemblage of fagots, furze and other fuel, also straw to be stacked and piled on the summit of Badbury Rings, so as the whole may take

fire instantly and the fire be maintained for two hours. The general direction if you will take the trouble of ordering the execution is that this beacon may be fired whenever the beacon off St Catherine's (Christchurch) is fired to the eastward, or whenever the beacons on Lytchet Heath or Woodbury Hill, are fired to the westward, but not from the demonstration of any coast signal.

In the final embodiment of a landscape, history – no less than geology – deposits its strata, layer by layer. In the record of the Channel coast of Wessex Hardy picks out the Napoleonic element for its emotional closeness to his generation. Through his poems and stories we can recognise it adding its depth of meaning to later fears of invasion and more recent departures of troopships.

In time of peace the coastal waters are a source of pleasure denied to inland folk. As a young man working in an architect's office, Hardy in 1869 lived in lodgings at Weymouth, where he rowed in the bay almost every summer evening and bathed 'at seven in the morning either on the pebblebeach towards Preston, or diving off from a boat'. There were steamboats operating from Weymouth, either as pleasure-trips on which 'there was dancing by moonlight, and where the couples would come suddenly down with a lurch into each other's arms', or as connections with other harbours in the vicinity. An early scene in *Desperate Remedies*, which Hardy was writing at this time, describes 'a popular local excursion by steamboat' from Weymouth to Lulworth Cove, during which harps and violins played music for dancing: Hardy himself made this excursion with his sister, Mary, in August 1868. Such vessels must have been a familiar sight in the Bay. In the poem 'On the Esplanade' Hardy captured the mood of a night at midsummer as he stood listening and watching just such a scene:

> Inside a window, open, with undrawn blind,
> There plays and sings
> A lady unseen a melody undefined:
> And where the moon flings
> Its shimmer a vessel crosses, whereon to the strings
> Plucked sweetly and low
> Of a harp, they dance.

The steamboat, like the railway train, offered new opportunities to people of Hardy's class and generation. In 1872, when he set off from London to visit Emma in Cornwall, he did so by way of the Irish Mail Packet Company's steamship *Avoca* to Plymouth, which afforded him an excellent view of the Wessex coast and useful material for a chapter in *A Pair of Blue Eyes*. In 1875 when he and Emma went from Bournemouth to select lodgings in Swanage they did so by sea. In 1882 they sailed from Weymouth to Cherbourg, and two years later Hardy and his brother crossed from Weymouth to Jersey, Guernsey and Sark: at the time he was writing the *Mayor of Casterbridge*, in which Henchard's visit to the Channel Islands is an important episode. A later novel, *The Well-Beloved*, similarly reflects Hardy's visit to Jersey. The Channel Islands had a particular interest for him as he liked to think that his Dorset ancestors came originally from Jersey.

This free open movement outwards from the inner recesses of the Wessex countryside is the other aspect of the coastal life, contrasting with the withdrawing defensive features. It introduces a cosmopolitan sense of wider horizons, which in Hardy's case was expressed most colourfully in two seaside resorts of very different character, Weymouth and Bournemouth — or as he named them, Budmouth and Sandbourne.

In his preface to *The Return of the Native*, which is set in the decade 1840–50, Hardy wrote that at that time 'Budmouth still retained sufficient afterglow from its Georgian gaiety and prestige to lend it an absorbing attractiveness to the romantic and imaginative soul of a lonely dweller inland'. He was himself such a 'soul': he could write with the authority of personal experience:

> As a rule, the word Budmouth meant fascination on Egdon. That Royal port and watering place, if truly mirrored in the minds of the heath folk, must have combined, in a charming and indescribable manner, a Carthaginian bustle of building with Tarentine luxuriousness and Baian health and beauty.

A remarkable place indeed, which the reddleman, Diggory Venn, described in simpler terms:

> 'Now Budmouth is a wonderful place — wonderful — a great salt sheening sea bending into the land like a bow — thousands of

gentlepeople walking up and down – bands of music playing –
officers by sea and officers by land walking among the rest – out
of every ten folk you meet nine of 'em in love.'

During his residence in Weymouth Hardy extended his own experience of falling in love, and out of love, on the evidence of the
poems he wrote at that time. He also recalled in after years his
membership of a dancing-class in Weymouth 'where a good deal of
flirtation went on'. This class, organised probably by two young
sisters – Mary Ann Elizabeth and Sarah Bartlett – was described by
Hardy as 'a gay gathering for dances and love-making by adepts of
both sexes'.

It is in such youthfully romantic terms that Hardy made some of
his most graphic sketches of Weymouth. After his first interview
with the architect who engaged him he stood on the Esplanade
opposite the Burdon Hotel and listened to the town band playing
Strauss waltzes: it was a scene in which he took a constant delight:

> The boats, the sands, the esplanade,
>   The laughing crowd;
>   Light-hearted, loud
> Greetings from some not ill-endowed;
>
> The evening sunlit cliffs, the talk,
>   Hailings and halts,
>   The keen sea-salts,
> The band, the Morgenblätter Waltz.

In his first published novel, *Desperate Remedies*, Hardy obviously
transferred scenes of Weymouth life directly and immediately to
the written page. His pleasure in sculling informs the scene in which
Edward Springrove and Cytherea declare their love while out rowing in the Bay. Sometimes her brother Owen accompanies them in
a threesome which appears again, and more personally, in the poem,
'Singing Lovers'.

> I rowed: the dimpled tide was at the turn,
> And mirth and moonlight spread upon the bay:
> There were two singing lovers in the stern;
>   But mine had gone away, –
>   Whither, I shunned to say!

The particular fascination of Victorian Weymouth owed much to
the fact that, in a provincial society, it preserved the contact with
the great world of high society that George III had given it. It was
fashionable. Agnes Grove's diaries in the 1880s show that Yeomanry Week in Weymouth at the end of May was a fixed point in
the social calendar of the aristocracy and landed gentry. The place
had an infectious glamour. In the young men's eyes every Budmouth girl was beautiful and every moment spent there was tinged
with adventure. To the inland cottagers it offered what Blackpool
offered to the milltowns of Lancashire. To the soldiery it was the
dream of home, remembered overseas:

> When we lay where Budmouth Beach is,
>   O, the girls were fresh as peaches,
> With their tall and tossing figures and their eyes of blue and brown!
>   And our hearts would ache with longing
>   As we paced from our sing-songing,
> With a smart *Clink! Clink!* up the Esplanade and down.

In later years, when Hardy looked at the middle-aged women in
Dorchester market he was struck with the thought that these were
the former beauties of an earlier generation who had been part of
the Budmouth scene:

> Are these the muslined pink young things to whom
>   We vowed and swore
> In nooks on summer Sundays by the Froom,
>   Or Budmouth shore?

In the present century the delights of Budmouth   as of most English
resorts – have tended to move down-market. The traditional
elegance has yielded to coarser tastes, but the general bustle and
excitement in pursuit of pleasure are in no way diminished – and
who would dare to deny that the girls are, as ever, 'fresh as
peaches'? Perhaps it is all rather more matter-of-fact, for ours is not
a romantic age – or is it simply that one's mood changes with each
change in the weather? When Hardy returned to Weymouth as a
married man, taking Emma with him to some holiday lodgings by
the harbour, they met a rainy spell: the scene as Hardy described
it, of an English seaside resort in a wet summer, is one to be
treasured by anybody who has shared a similar experience:

133

Their time in the port was mostly wet; the excursion-steamer bell ringing persistently, and nobody going on board except an unfortunate boys' school that had come eight miles by train that morning to spend a happy day by the sea. The rain goes into their baskets of provisions, and runs out a strange mixture of cake-juice and mustard-water, but they try to look as if they were enjoying it – all except the pale thin assistant-master who has come with them, and whose face is tragic with his responsibilities . . . Two adventurous visitors have emerged from their lodgings as far as the doorway, where they stand in their waterproof cloaks and goloshes, saying cheerfully, 'The air will do us good, and we can change as soon as we come in.' Young men rush to the bathing machines in ulsters, and the men engaged in loading a long-voyage steamer lose all patience, and say: 'I'm blanked, if it goes on much longer like this we shall be rotted alive!'

Gloucester Lodge, which subsequently became the Gloucester Hotel, was built for the Duke of Gloucester in about 1780, when the medicinal value of sea-bathing was the new craze. The arrival of George III and the royal family in 1789 established the town as the *doyen* of Wessex's seaside resorts. Bournemouth, by contrast, is the *parvenu* whose boomtime had to wait for a newer craze – the medicinal value of pine-scented air. This health-giving feature was discovered by a London doctor who despatched his wealthy clients to inhale the odours of the new resort that Squire Tregonwell had founded on the deserted heathland between the ports of Christchurch and Poole.

When Hardy was born there were barely a couple of dozen buildings where Bournemouth now stands. Seven years later Lady Stanley, giving news of her daughter 'Ally' (Alethea), wrote in a letter: 'Ally is at Bourn Mouth and she likes the place very much, so quiet and good bathing and Poole, their post town, so primitive'.

It was in 1810 that Lewis Tregonwell visited the district and, in the following year, built a summer residence there. The Groves of Ferne were close friends of the Tregonwells, and Helen Tregonwell stayed at Ferne in January and again in April 1811: at the end of May Charlotte Grove wrote in her diary: 'A party of pleasure to Bourne Cliff. Mr. Tregonwell's new house – dined on cold meat in the house. The sea shore beautiful'.

134

Development was slow. In 1826 a blackcock was shot on what became the site of the parish church, St Peter's. In 1851 Sir Percy Shelley, the poet's son, came to live at Boscombe manor and the poet's widow was buried at St Peter's in that year. The population was then still under 700. Understandably therefore the sudden irruption of wealth and fashion in what had been a wilderness captured Hardy's imagination by its novelty. 'A Mediterranean lounging-place on the English Channel' was his description of it. When Rosa Halborough, in 'A Tragedy of Two Ambitions', is to be groomed for social success she is sent to 'a high-class school at Sandbourne'. In *The Hand of Ethelberta*, published in 1876, there is a sketch of the rapidly growing town: Christopher Julian is 'directed to the outskirts, and into a fir plantation where drives and intersecting roads had been laid out, and where new villas had

Bournemouth: from the west cliff

135

sprung up like mushrooms'. Fifteen years later when *Tess of the d'Urbervilles* was published, Angel Clare commented, 'Sandbourne has become a large place, they say' – on hearing that Tess had gone to live there.

> This fashionable watering-place, with its eastern and its western stations, its piers, its groves of pines, its promenades, and its covered gardens, was, to Angel Clare, like a fairy place suddenly created by the stroke of a wand, and allowed to get a little dusty. An outlying eastern tract of the enormous Egdon Waste was close at hand, yet on the very verge of that tawny piece of antiquity such a glittering novelty as this pleasure city had chosen to spring up. Within the space of a mile from its outskirts every irregularity of the soil was prehistoric, every channel an undisturbed British trackway; not a sod having been turned there since the days of the Caesars. Yet the exotic had grown here, suddenly as the prophet's gourd.

It was doubtless this exotic quality in 1890 which attracted Hardy's pen to 'Sandbourne' as the place of sin and shame and ultimately of murder to which Alec d'Urberville took Tess as his mistress.

The coast east of Bournemouth made surprisingly little impression on Hardy, despite its varied scenery and its historical associations. The New Forest littoral and Christchurch Bay, with the estuaries of the Beaulieu and Lymington rivers, have a claim to be mentioned in any account of Wessex. Christchurch itself, with its magnificent priory on the edge of the lagoon made by the twin estuaries of Stour and Avon, seems ideally suited to support a Hardyesque story or poem. It was a notable centre of smuggling: as a schoolboy in the 1790s Richard Warner watched a procession of twenty or thirty waggons, accompanied by two or three hundred horsemen carrying kegs of spirits, 'winding deliberately and with most picturesque and imposing effect along the skirts of Hengistbury Head in their way towards the wild country to the northwest of Christchurch'.

The superb view from the summit of Hengistbury Head, looking over Christchurch harbour, recalls the very similar prospect – though on a larger scale – of Poole Harbour seen from the Purbeck heights of Nine Barrow Down, as Hardy described it in *The Hand of Ethelberta*, looking first at the harbour and Brownsea Island and then at the open sea beyond Studland Bay:

> Silver sunbeams lighted up a many-armed inland sea which stretched round an island with fir-trees and gorse, and amid brilliant crimson heaths wherein white paths and roads occasionally met the eye in dashes and zigzags like flashes of lightning. Outside, where the broad Channel appeared, a berylline and opalized variegation of ripples, currents, deeps, and shallows lay as fair under the sun as a New Jerusalem, the shores being of gleaming sand.

A century ago the further shore of the harbour was not dominated by a monstrous power-station and the industrialised skyline that now leads the eastward urban sprawl to Bournemouth: even so it is not difficult to recapture the essence of the scene that so impressed Ethelberta. In size the harbour is reputed to be exceeded only by that of Sydney. As a natural haven it was developed on the Hamworthy shore as a port by the Romans, with a road link to Badbury Rings. Its long maritime history includes a prominent role in the Newfoundland trade and it is this period in the annals of *Swanage*

'Havenpool' that Hardy selected for the story entitled 'To Please his Wife'.

On the Isle of Purbeck Hardy was on familiar ground. Swanage and Corfe Castle were places that he knew with an intimacy that set them apart from other places further afield to which he had been little more than a brief and casual visitor. The gateway to Purbeck is Wareham, and Wareham is encompassed by the twin streams of Hardy's boyhood – the Frome and the Piddle, which both enter Poole Harbour in little more than a mile subsequently. The Valley of the Great Dairies comes to its climax and its conclusion, therefore, in the waters of the Wareham channel; and the southern flank of Egdon Heath similarly is dramatically, abruptly, halted by the harbour, the sea and the barrier of the Purbeck hills.

Purbeck is a fine example of the geological variety that can be compressed into a small area of the Dorset landscape: chalk, clay, limestone, sand and shale combine here in scenery which can be rugged at one moment and gentle the next. Stone and marble, oil

Corfe Castle

Corfe Castle: the keep

and ball clay are the mineral riches that support its long history of human activity. The causeway through the Corfe gap to Wareham was its one land-link with the larger world. Its other connections were by sea. Swanage – Hardy's 'Knollsea' – is Purbeck's only town and it is a late-comer, developed in the last hundred years as a conventional seaside-resort. When Hardy lived there, in 1875, Swanage was still a village – as he described it in *The Hand of Ethelberta*:

> Knollsea was a seaside village lying snug within two headlands as between a finger and thumb. Everybody in the parish who was not a boatman was a quarrier, unless he were the gentleman who owned half the property and had been a quarryman, or the other gentleman who owned the other half, and had been to sea.
> The knowledge of the inhabitants was of the same special sort as their pursuits. The quarrymen in white fustian understood practical geology, the laws and accidents of dips, faults and cleavage, far better than the ways of the world and mammon; the seafaring men in Guernsey frocks had a clearer notion of Alexandria, Constantinople, the Cape, and the Indies than of any inland

town in their own country. This, for them, consisted of a busy portion, the Channel, where they lived and laboured, and a dull portion, the vague unexplored miles of interior at the back of the ports, which they seldom thought of.

The cliffs and headlands of Purbeck and the tempestuous winter seas that beat against them and filled the air with spray had a strong effect on Hardy. With Emma he walked daily on the cliffs and along the shore: for both of them the rearing waves must have aroused memories of the Cornish cliffs during the days of their courtship in the preceding years. In a note made at the time, Hardy recalled an evening when they sat together, just after sunset, on a stone under a wall, listening to the background roar of the sea and the song of a bird nearby – 'The sounds are two, and only two. On the left Durlstone Head roaring high and low, like a giant asleep. On the right a thrush. Above the bird hangs the new moon, and a steady planet'.

They had been married less than a year and had as yet no settled home. The notebook entry suggests a closely shared and deeply felt mood which found a more permanent expression in the poem, 'Once at Swanage':

> The spray sprang up across the cusps of the moon,
> And all its light loomed green
> As a witch-flame's weirdsome sheen
> At the minute of an incantation scene;
> And it greened our gaze – that night at demilune.
>
> Roaring high and roaring low was the sea
> Behind the headland shores:
> It symboled the slamming of doors,
> Or a regiment hurrying over hollow floors. . . .
> And there we two stood, hands clasped; I and she!

Just as *A Pair of Blue Eyes* is the novel of the north coast of Cornwall and *The Well-Beloved* of Portland, so *The Hand of Ethelberta* is the novel of Purbeck. Ethelberta's story starts at Wareham ('Anglebury') and ends at 'Enckworth', the family seat of the man she marries, Lord Mountclere. 'Enckworth' is freely based on Encombe House, which had a particular interest for Hardy because of its connection with his native village. The house was bought in the

St Aldhelm's Head, Purbeck

1730s for John Pitt by his father George, who had married an heiress of Kingston Maurward: the bust of George Pitt, made by his son John, is in Stinsford church and would have been a familiar sight to the young Thomas Hardy. John Pitt probably rebuilt or largely modified the house, which passed in the nineteenth century to the Scott family, its present owners. It occupies a most attractive setting beside a lake in a narrow valley between Swyre Head and Houns-tout Cliff.

In the final stages of the novel Hardy paints a seascape which emphasises the turbulent and perilous nature of Dorset's coastal waters, from Purbeck to Portland Bill. The steamer *Spruce*, unable to berth at Knollsea because of stormy seas, must turn back to Sandbourne. This entailed keeping well offshore to avoid the Foreland at the northern end of Swanage Bay:

> The direction and increase of the wind had made it necessary to keep the vessel still further to sea on their return than in going, that they might clear without risk the windy, sousing, thwacking, basting, scourging Jack Ketch of a corner called Old-Harry Point, which lay about halfway along their track, and stood, with its detached posts and stumps of white rock, like a skeleton's lower jaw, grinning at British navigation. Here strong currents and cross currents were beginning to interweave their scrolls and meshes, the water rising behind them in tumultous heaps, and slamming against the fronts and angles of cliff, whence it flew into the air like clouds of flour.

From Swanage to Weymouth the Channel coast is remarkable for its variety and picturesque contrasts. Treves, who lived at Lulworth, knew it well and was prepared to match it against any equivalent length of England's coast-line, for reasons that he set out with precision:

Ballard Point, Swanage: Bournemouth in the distance

> In this sea line are cliffs of jagged rocks, sheer as a bastion wall, as well as green lawns which creep lazily to the water's edge. There are wide, open bays, and fissured sea-echoing chines. There are round coves, inlets reached through arched rocks, level sands, and moaning caves. There are beaches of shingle, of pebbles, of colossal boulders, and of the clay of crumbling banks; precipices of every colour, from the white of chalk to the black

of the shale; and walls of stone streaked with tints of yellow, buff, or red.

It is a coast that Hardy touches at several points in poem and story – at Ringstead Bay and Durdle Door and of course Lulworth, where Sergeant Troy was thought to have drowned, in *Far from the Madding Crowd*, and John Keats's brief landing there in 1820 inspired the poem 'At Lulworth Cove a Century Back'. At Osmington the chalk figure of George III on horseback, cut in the downland turf, signals the approach of Weymouth Bay, Portland Harbour and the Chesil Beach.

Portland, like the other stone 'island', Purbeck, appealed strongly to Hardy. 'That Gibraltar of Wessex' he called it: a peninsula 'carved by Time out of a single stone', to which he gave the fictional name 'the Isle of Slingers'. Prominent among its inhabitants are the

Portland Castle

quarrymen, the prison-warders and the Services personnel who add a stern masculine style to a landscape that Nature endowed with an unrelenting grimness. This steep-sided rock of grudging aspect consists, as Hardy describes it in *The Well-Beloved*, of 'houses above houses, one man's doorstep rising behind his neighbour's chimney, the gardens hung up by one edge to the sky, the vegetables growing on apparently almost vertical planes'.

In the quarries the limestone blocks are still torn out of the core of the island and sent away, as they were when Wren used them in St Paul's. Hardy liked to watch the freight trains from Portland passing through Dorchester. When he was eighty-seven his second wife made a note after one of their usual little walks along the cinder-path beside the railway line: 'We stood and watched a goods train carrying away huge blocks of Portland stone as we have done so many times. He seems never tired of watching these stone-laden

145

trucks. He said he thought that the shape of Portland would be changed in the course of years by the continual cutting away of its surface'.

Portland's connection with the mainland is by way of the extra-ordinary ridge of pebbles which encloses the water of the Fleet as far as Abbotsbury and continues as a beach to Burton Bradstock. This is the Chesil Bank or Chesil Beach. Its link with Weymouth used to be by ferry, which is now replaced by a permanent road-way. The stones of which it is composed range from large pebbles at the Portland end to a fine shingle at Burton Bradstock. It is claimed that a local man, cast up on the Chesil in darkness, could estimate his position from the size of the stones, so evenly precise is the gradation of size from one end to the other. Its greatest dimensions are at the Portland end — about 200 yards wide and rising to a maximum of over forty feet above highwater mark. In rough weather the sea will break its waves over the Bank and many a vessel has been trapped and wrecked here in what is known with good reason as Deadman's Bay.

Some of the more spectacular calamities on the Chesil Beach have

West Bay,
Bridport

passed into local folklore and would have figured in the hearthside conversations of Hardy's elders that he listened to as a boy. In the year before he was born, a vessel of 500 tons was lifted by high seas clean over the bank into the calmer waters of Portland Roads, while nine other craft were being driven aground and smashed to pieces. In 1795 the bodies of over 200 drowned men were buried on the Chesil Beach where they were found. The great storm which raged along the coast in 1824 swept away part of the little village of Chesilton, between Weymouth and Portland – an event which Hardy brings into *The Well-Beloved*. His knowledge of it was based on a visit he made in 1879 when he noted: 'As to the ruined walls in the low part of Chesil, a woman says the house was washed down in the November gale of 1824. The owner never rebuilt it, but emigrated with his family. She says that in her house one person was

The Chesil Bank, with Portland Bill beyond

147

Lyme Regis

drowned (they were all in bed except the fishermen) and next door two people. It was about four in the morning that the wave came.'

On this occasion the Bank was breached and at Abbotsbury the Earl of Ilchester's swannery was flooded to a depth of over 22 feet. Normally the swans breed securely within the calm water of the Fleet which the Chesil Bank encloses and protects, while terns nest on the Bank itself. Rising behind the coast is the exhilarating stretch of downland which forms the background of Lyme Bay. The road westwards from Dorchester to Bridport and beyond was a favourite drive of Hardy's and needs no recommendation to anyone who has once enjoyed travelling along it. A prominent landmark is Maiden Castle, the scene of the story 'A Tryst at an Ancient Earthwork'. Blackdown Hill provides another and less appealing landmark, the Hardy monument – the Hardy in question being Nelson's Hardy, the Admiral whose home was nearby, at Portisham. There is no accounting for the design of his monument, which seems to have been intended originally as a chimney for a crematorium. His memory is preserved in a kindlier way in *The Trumpet-Major* and *The Dynasts*.

Bridport and West Bay were drawn by Hardy in the short story 'Fellow Townsmen', where Bridport is 'Port Bredy', the little town with a worldwide reputation for its ropes and nets. In his description of the ropewalks he portrays the rope-makers 'walking backwards, overhung by appletrees and bushes, and intruded on by cows and calves, as if trade had established itself there at considerable inconvenience to Nature'. The town itself was so jammed into a narrow valley through the surrounding downland that 'the shepherd on the east hill could shout out lambing intelligence to the shepherd on the west hill, over the intervening town chimneys.' West Bay is Bridport's harbour and at first glance might seem to be 'a beginning made by Nature herself of a perfect harbour'; but every attempt to develop it has been frustrated by the tides which choke it with sand and shingle.

Westwards the Channel coast stretches away beyond Golden Cap and Lyme Regis to the shores of Devon, to culminate in Plymouth Sound and the grey roofs huddled about the Hoe. It was here that Hardy's journey down-Channel ended on board the *Avoca* in 1872, after a sunlit dawn vision of the Devon coast:

All up the coast, prominences singled themselves out from recesses. Then a rosy sky spread over the eastern sea and behind the low line of the land, flinging its livery in dashes upon the thin airy clouds in that direction. Every projection on the land seemed now so many fingers anxious to catch a little of the liquid light thrown so prodigally over the sky . . . The bluff and bare contours of Start Point caught the brightest, earliest glow of all and so also did the sides of its white lighthouse, perched upon a shelf in its precipitous front like a mediaeval saint in a niche. Their lofty neighbour Bolt Head on the left remained as yet ungilded, and retained its gray.

Then up came the sun, as it were in jerks, just to seaward of the easternmost point of land, flinging out a Jacob's-ladder path of light from itself . . . The inferior dignitaries of the shore – Froward Point, Berry Head, and Prawle – all had acquired their share of illumination ere this, and at length the very smallest protuberance of wave, cliff, or inlet, even to the innermost recesses of the lovely valley of the Dart, had its portion; and sunlight, now the common possession of all, ceased to be the wonderful and coveted thing it had been a short half hour before.

After breakfast, Plymouth arose into view, and grew distincter to their nearing vision, the Breakwater appearing like a streak of phosphoric light upon the surface of the sea.

CHAPTER NINE

Forest and Downland

The western parts of Wessex – Devon and Cornwall – are strikingly distinct in character from the 'heartland'. On the eastern side there is a greater homogeneity. The chalk downland of Dorset extends into the comparable landscapes of the Marlborough Downs and Cranborne Chase. The Vale of Blackmore finds an echo in the greensand of the Vale of Pewsey. The heathy waste of Egdon reaches across in harmony to the heaths of the New Forest with no other interruption than the river valleys of Stour and Avon.

This is not to gainsay that there are important distinctions of emphasis and detail, even in landscapes that appear superficially similar. The archaeological riches of the Wiltshire chalk set it apart from any other area. The New Forest and Cranborne Chase taken together represent the last part of England in which the old laws of the Forest for the preservation of deer for hunting operated. Newmarket Heath lies far outside Hardy's Wessex but the training gallops of the Wiltshire and Berkshire downs are not less hallowed in racing circles. One way and another there is plenty to observe and enjoy to the east of Somerset and Dorset.

The Dorset border, as Hardy knew it, embraced Poole but rejected Bournemouth. It has since been moved to create a larger county by annexing Bournemouth and also Christchurch. Inland, the valley of the Stour offers itself as a frontier of a more durably historical sort. King John made it the boundary of Cranborne Chase from Manston through Blandford to Wimborne, and it creates a useful new grouping by turning its back on the Great Dairies, the Little Dairies, the rivers of the Poole basin, Purbeck, and even 'Casterbridge' itself, as 'Melchester' – Hardy's 'tall-spired town' of Salisbury – begins to make its presence felt in the east.

The Stour is one of several rivers which define the territory of Cranborne Chase. The Nadder provides its northern limit, the Avon its eastern, and the Allen and the Crane much of its southern boundary. There are no towns within the Chase: they are on its borders – Wimborne, Blandford, Shaftesbury, Wilton, Salisbury, Fordingbridge and Ringwood. The last two, bridging the Avon, are linking gateways to the New Forest. In *Two on a Tower* Hardy gives this picture of the Chase – 'a country of ragged woodland, which, though intruded on by the plough at places, remained largely intact from prehistoric times, and still abounded with yews of gigantic growth and oaks tufted with mistletoe'.

Its woodlands remained 'largely intact', as did those of the New Forest, because the forest laws of 'vert and venison' protected not only the deer but their requirements also of food and shelter. No tree could be felled, no wooded area cleared, without the consent of the Lord of the Chase – even though he, or she, might not own the particular piece of land involved. The lord's right to preserve the deer was paramount everywhere within the bounds. It was in origin a royal prerogative and in the case of the New Forest it remained so from William the Conqueror to Queen Victoria. Cranborne Chase, however, passed out of the monarch's hands finally when James I ceded his lordship to Robert Cecil, Viscount Cranborne and later Earl of Salisbury. In private hands it became a privilege, a benefit, to be bought and sold; as such it was finally acquired by the Pitt family, raised to the peerage as the Barons Rivers.

In the lifetime of Hardy's father the forest laws were enforced in Cranborne Chase, in the face of growing resentment and opposition from the farming interests. Modern methods of cultivation were hampered by the Chase laws, and the predominance of the deer encouraged poaching and a general lawlessness which brought the coastal smugglers into an unholy alliance with the deer-stealers. A document of 1791 described the Chase as 'a nursery for and a temptation of all kinds of vice, profligacy and immorality', where whole parishes had become 'nests of deer-stealers, bred to it by their parents'.

It was not until 1830 that the Chase was disfranchised by a special act of Parliament and the 'lordship' – the last to be held by a British subject – was extinguished. Only Queen Victoria now retained this right, in respect of the New Forest; and in 1851 she divested herself of it. The preservation of deer, except on one's own land – in an ornamental park, for instance – was ended. Hardy therefore witnessed the final stage of a traditional practice which had moulded a substantial part of the Wessex landscape. I often wonder whether it was a poet's instinct or a deliberate symbolism which made him select this area as the suitably dramatic background for the violence and fear in Tess's life, and the ultimate hunting of her. 'The oldest wood in England' is Alec d'Urberville's description of the Chase, as he prepares to seduce her there; and Hardy emphasises this in the first impression of the scene when Tess makes her initial visit to the d'Urberville mansion:

> Far behind the corner of the house – which rose like a geranium bloom against the subdued colours around – stretched the soft azure landscape of The Chase – a truly venerable tract of forest land, one of the few remaining woodlands in England of undoubted primaeval date, wherein Druidical mistletoe was still found on aged oaks, and where enormous yew-trees, not planted by the hand of man, grew as they had grown when they were pollarded for bows.

The mention of 'Druidical mistletoe' seems already to excite anticipation of the scene which concludes the hunt, at Stonehenge.

The flight of Angel and Tess from 'Sandbourne' through the New Forest is made in a lightly sketched context. The scene is neatly captured in the phrase 'this half-woodland, half-moorland part of the country' but very little detail is added. In a letter written in 1897 to the *Saturday Review* Hardy mentioned 'New Forest vistas near Brockenhurst' as one of five particularly pleasing scenes in Wessex, but he made no attempt to incorporate any characteristic Forest scenery in *Tess*. The house where the two fugitives spent a few idyllic days of loving tranquillity together is usually considered to be based on Moyle's Court, near Rockford: at one time the home of Alice, Lady Lisle, whom Judge Jeffreys condemned so barbarously, it is now a school. By naming it 'Bramshurst Court' Hardy seemed to want to turn speculation towards Bramshaw.

He himself liked to picnic in the New Forest. Driving back from Queen's College, Oxford, in 1923, he and his wife had lunch 'in a grassy glade in the New Forest in the simple way that Hardy so much preferred'. It was perhaps this occasion which prompted one of his last poems, 'Throwing a Tree', which he subtitled 'New Forest': it describes the way two foresters undertake the felling of a tree with axes, ropes and a two-handled saw:

Then, lastly, the living mast sways, further sways: with a shout
Job and Ike rush aside. Reached the end of its long staying powers
The tree crashes downward: it shakes all its neighbours
    throughout,
And two hundred years' steady growth has been ended in less
    than two hours.

For Hardy the New Forest was primarily a place to visit briefly, whereas Cranborne Chase he knew more intimately. At the western end he had lived in two of the Stour valley towns, Sturminster Newton and Wimborne. The two northern extremities touched towns that had a special place in his affections, Salisbury and Shaftesbury. The roads that cross the Chase were similarly among his favourites. *The Life* records that in 1919 'on his birthday in June he did what he had long intended to do – took his wife and sister to Salisbury by the old road which had been travelled by his and their forefathers in their journeys to London – via Blandford, Woodyates Inn, and Harnham Hill, whence Constable had painted his famous view of the cathedral'.

This road, now the A354, was the Great Western Turnpike. Constructed in the eighteenth century to meet the growing demands of coach-travel, it replaced the earlier road from Weymouth to London which took a more southerly route, through Cranborne and Martin to reach Salisbury. An attempt was made to revive this old route as part of a new turnpike from Poole through Wimborne to Martin and ultimately Salisbury: this too was a favourite of Hardy's. In 'Barbara of the House of Grebe' the road (now the B3078) is the link between the seats of Sir John Grebe at Canford and Lord Uplandtowers at Wimborne St Giles; and Hardy describes it in surprising detail:

The seats of the two families were about ten miles apart, the way between them lying along the now old, then new, turnpike-road connecting Havenpool [*Poole*] and Warborne [*Wimborne*] with the city of Melchester [*Salisbury*]: a road which, though only

153

a branch from what was known as the Great Western Highway, is probably, even at present, as it has been for the last hundred years, one of the finest examples of a macadamized turnpike track that can be found in England.

The stretch of the Stour from Manston to Wimborne is marked impressively by the fortified hill-tops of prehistory – Hod Hill and Hambledon, Spetisbury and Buzbury, even Badbury Rings barely a couple of miles from the riverbank. Hardy 'nearly got lost in the dark inside the earthworks on Hambledon Hill' after a visit to Shroton Fair; later he commented, 'A man might go round and round all night in such a place'. No less impressive are the mediaeval bridges – Crawford Bridge at Spetisbury and White Mill Bridge at Sturminster Marshall.

Of the two riverside towns Blandford ('Shottsford') drew from Farmer Cawtree in *The Woodlanders* the enigmatic pronouncement, after his visit there, that 'Shottsford is Shottsford still – you can't victual your carcase there unless you've got money; and you can't buy a cup of genuine there, whether or no . . .' A visitor today, chancing perhaps to be of a more generous spirit, might be pleased to find much of the town's eighteenth-century architecture surviving contemporary pressures. A traditional craft that interested Hardy was painting on glass. John Aubrey, as a schoolboy in Blandford, used to visit the shop and furnaces of a glasspainter named Harding who died in 1643, aged about 83. In 'Barbara of the House of Grebe', the ill-fated lover Edmond Willowes is described as 'a young fellow of Shottsford-Forum' who is the son or grandson of 'the last of the old glass-painters in that place, where (as you may know) the art lingered on when it had died out in every other part of England'.

Wimborne engaged Hardy more thoroughly. He and Emma lived in the town from 1881 to 1883, and it was here that *Two on a Tower* was written. The young hero of the novel, Swithin St Cleeve, was educated at Wimborne ('Warborne') Grammar School: when Lady Constantine enquires about his schooling, her informant – Amos Fry – pays the school this startling tribute: 'A place where they draw up young gam'sters' brains like rhubarb under a ninepenny pan, my lady, excusing my common way. They hit so much larning into en that 'a could talk like the day of Pentecost'.

The New Forest, near Lyndhurst

Living in the little house called 'Llanherne' at Wimborne Hardy enjoyed its well-kept garden, with all sorts of old-fashioned flowers, and fruit in profusion. When the weather permitted he liked to do his literary work sitting under the vine on the stable-wall, 'which for want of training hangs in long arms over my head nearly to the ground. The sun tries to shine through the great leaves, making a green light on the paper'.

Much to his taste was Wimborne Minster, Saxon in origin and still retaining early Norman features in its fabric – a massive, dark, brooding presence, with a touch of gaiety in the famous Quarter-Jack of its animated clock. As he copied the architectural detail of the Minster in a pencil-drawing Hardy began to formulate a poem about it:

> How smartly the quarters of the hour march by
>   That the jack-o'-clock never forgets;
> Ding-dong; and before I have traced a cusp's eye,
>   Or got the true twist of the ogee over,
>   A double ding-dong ricochetts.

In a lighter vein he wrote 'The Levelled Churchyard', which made a satirical comment on the way the minster's burial-ground had been tidied up, with scant regard for the identities of the dead. Headstones were removed and mounds levelled in such a wholesale fashion that the orderly patterns of interment were jumbled up in inextricable confusion. A ghostly voice complains in the poem that 'Teetotal Tommy's' headstone has been transferred to the grave of a roaring drunkard, and that

> 'Here's not a modest maiden elf
>   But dreads the final Trumpet,
> Lest half of her should rise herself,
>   And half some sturdy strumpet!'

From Wimborne the road to Cranborne passes the Horton Inn – the 'Lornton Inn' where the post-chaise had waited to play its part in the elopement of Barbara Grebe. The inn continues to be a prominent and welcome landmark on the erstwhile turnpike but it no longer fits Hardy's description of it as 'the rendezvous of many a daring poacher for operations in the adjoining forest', if only because the forest has largely disappeared. Holt Forest, Holt Common and Horton Heath together formed a wild appendage to the southern limit of Cranborne Chase, being in effect a part of the Egdon heathland extending between Stour and Avon to join the New Forest. The many goodly oaks that Michael Drayton celebrated here in the early seventeenth century are no more. There are conifer plantations here and there; much of the vicinity has been reclaimed for agriculture; and increasingly the developer brings the coastal urbanisation deeper inland. Horton's other landmark, besides its inn, is the observatory tower built in the eighteenth century by Humphry Sturt.

Any poacher one might meet in the neighbourhood today would be very different from the conventional idea of the quiet countryman intent on knocking over a pheasant or a rabbit for the pot. He is equally likely to come from town or city, driving a light van: his quarry is probably deer, but he may be engaged in the shameful trade of robbing the nests of rare and endangered species of birds, for sale to egg-collectors.

The customary indulgence extended to poachers makes a distinction between downright theft – as it would be if farm-animals were involved – and the uncertain 'crime' of trespass in the pursuit of a wild animal which belongs permanently to nobody. Trespass was so often linked with the unjust and unpopular system of enclosure that it was regarded lightly. When Victorian men of property became ever stricter in the enforcement of the laws protecting their possessions a voice as mild even as William Barnes's was raised in protest, in one of his vernacular poems:

> Vor to breed the young fox or the heäre
> We can gi'e up whole eäcres o' ground;
> But the greens be a-grudged, vor to rear
> Our young children up healthy an' sound,
> Why, there woont be a-left the next age
> A green spot where their veet can goo vree:
> An' the goocoo wull soon be committed to cage
> Vor a trespass in zomebody's tree.

The smuggler similarly was something of a folk-hero since he could claim that he robbed only the tax-gatherer, for whom tears are rarely shed. For Hardy poacher and smuggler were indeterminate figures, moving with nocturnal stealth about their business. The

157

poem 'Winter Night in Woodland', which he subtitled 'Old Time', shows them in noncommital terms as part of the Wessex scene:

> With clap-nets and lanterns off start the bird-baiters,
> In trim to make raids on the roosts in the copse,
> Where they beat the boughs artfully, while their awaiters
> Grow heavy at home over divers warm drops.
> The poachers, with swingels, and matches of brimstone, outcreep
> To steal upon pheasants and drowse them a-perch and asleep.

> Out there, on the verge, where a path wavers through,
> Dark figures, filed singly, thrid quickly the view,
> Yet heavily laden: land-carriers are they
> In the hire of the smugglers from some nearest bay.
> Each bears his two 'tubs', slung across, one in front, one behind,
> To a further snug hiding, which none but themselves are to find.

The poacher's swingel was a kind of flail 'loaded' with strips of iron. The traditional link of eel-skin, connecting the handle to the beater, was replaced by a short length of chain so that a sword could not sever the joints. Hardy refers again to this brutal weapon in *The Mayor of Casterbridge* during his description of 'Peter's Finger', the disreputable inn in Mixen Lane:

> The thunder of bowls echoed from the backyard; swingels hung behind the blower of the chimney; and ex-poachers and ex-gamekeepers, whom squires had persecuted without a cause, sat elbowing each other — men who in past times had met in fights under the moon, till lapse of sentences on the one part, and loss of favour and expulsion from service on the other, brought them here together to a common level, where they sat calmly discussing old times.

Added to the swingel as part of the poacher's battledress were the cap and jack. In Cranborne Chase these were a protective helmet ingeniously made of woven straw on a withy framework; and a thickly quilted and padded jacket. A man thus protected and armed was a formidable opponent — as I can testify, having once donned cap and jack myself and handled a swingel preserved with some pride by the descendants of one who fought at the battle of Bloody Shard Gate in the latter part of the eighteenth century.

The romantic view of such affrays tends not to dwell on the severe maimings and occasional deaths that resulted. On Chettle Common, for instance, in 1780 it was blows from swingels that smashed one keeper's knee-cap and broke three ribs of another who subsequently died, while one of the deer-stealers had a hand severed by a keeper's cutlass. These confrontations reached such a pitch in Cranborne Chase that a party of dragoons, planning to ambush a train of fifty smugglers as they passed through the woods with laden pack-horses, were defeated and deprived of their horses and weapons.

Hardy's grandparents may well have heard news of the poacher who was killed in 1791 in a fight with keepers near Rushmore Lodge, and it was such tales that stored the mind of the young Thomas. The short story 'The Distracted Preacher' owes its authentic details of smuggling methods to the reminiscences of an ex-smuggler who worked in his latter years for Hardy's father: this man had been a 'land-carrier' bearing his two tubs slung over his shoulders, 'one in front, one behind'.

Cranborne Manor House

159

In 'The Distracted Preacher' the landing-points for contraband shipped from Cherbourg were Ringstead Bay and Lulworth Cove, and the Preventive officers were based at Weymouth. Larger cargoes probably involved the fishermen and seamen of Poole and Christchurch: the desolate heathland between the two harbours was well suited to the movement of pack-horses from the shore to the fastnesses of Cranborne Chase, where goods could be hidden for despatch at a safe opportunity to the principal black markets of Bristol and London.

Cranborne itself was named 'Chaseborough' by Hardy and described by him as 'a decayed market-town'. King John had had his hunting-lodge here and it was the administrative centre of the Chase, serving the same purpose as the monarch's house in Lyndhurst did for the New Forest. When it passed to James I's 'little beagle', Robert Cecil, Cranborne manorhouse was transformed into the Jacobean masterpiece which is still the property of the Cecil family. It lost its administrative function, however, when the lordship of the Chase passed to the Earls of Shaftesbury and later the Barons Rivers — the business of the Chase court being transferred successively to Wimborne St Giles and Rushmore Lodge. Cranborne's decline was accelerated when the Great Western Turnpike bypassed it, and the railway later did the same.

For Tess and the other farmworkers at 'Trantridge' the attractions offered by 'Chaseborough', humble though they might be, were good enough for a Saturday night's outing after a hard-working week; and so they walked the two or three miles that were the necessary preliminary to the pleasures of drinking and dancing. They were a hard-drinking lot, and a fair or a market-day brought some rough characters into the place. The undercurrent of menace and fear in the atmosphere of the Chase – so different from her home at Marlott – is reflected in Tess's indecision while she waits for companionship on the walk home:

> She became restless and uneasy; yet, having waited so long, it was necessary to wait longer; on account of the fair the roads were dotted with roving characters of possibly ill intent; and, though not fearful of measurable dangers, she feared the unknown. Had she been near Marlott she would have had less dread.

'Chaseborough' today is tranquil enough. 'The Flower-de-Luce' that Tess knew is easily recognised as the Fleur de Lys. As for 'Trantridge' (Pentridge) – the 'three-mile walk, along a dry white road' to the village on the downland crest will not reveal 'The Slopes', where Alec d'Urberville lived with his widowed mother, since it is wholly fictitious. The village of Pentridge has lost the road that used to pass through it and has accordingly become a *cul de sac* of such impenetrable solitude that Cranborne does still seem, by contrast, to be the buzzing, Saturday-night-out sort of place that Tess found it – though nowadays the more energetic citizens of Pentridge may seek their entertainment in Salisbury or Bournemouth.

A plaque in Pentridge church commemorates the connection of the parish with the family of the poet Robert Browning. Hardy, who liked and admired Browning, was interested in this association with Pentridge and more specifically with the Woodyates Inn on the Blandford-Salisbury road. When he visited the inn Hardy recalled that Browning's great-grandfather had been its landlord: it became famous as a stopping-place for the royal family during George III's visits to Weymouth. It closed when the railways replaced the coaches, but the revival of road traffic by the motorcar suggested to Hardy that the inn, which in 1919 'still retained its genial hostelry appearance', might have prospered again. It did not do so, however, and was demolished in 1967.

Woodyates is also worth mentioning in quite a different context. It stands at the point where the Roman road from Badbury to Old Sarum passes through the massive earthwork known as Bokerley Dyke, and it was here that General Augustus Pitt-Rivers made what is perhaps his most celebrated excavation, in the course of which he founded the modern method of scientific archaeology. He was able to demonstrate how and approximately when the road had been blocked, re-opened and finally blocked again in the times of uncertainty when Roman rule was failing and the early Saxon invasions threatened.

Pitt-Rivers's excavations in Cranborne Chase were of obvious interest to Hardy and a friendship developed between the two men. They were fellow-members of the Athenaeum. Hardy dined at Pitt-Rivers's London house and subsequently visited the family 'seat' at Rushmore, near Tollard Royal in a remote part of Cranborne Chase. Pitt-Rivers felt he had a mission to educate the masses – particularly

161

in the new scientific thought of geologists, archaeologists and evolutionists. He therefore created a museum on revolutionary principles at Tollard Farnham and planned to attract the masses to it by 'other inducements'. As he explained in an address to the Society of Arts in 1891, 'I have formed a recreation ground, called the Larmer Grounds, where my private band plays every Sunday in the summer months from three to five'. Known also as the Larmer Tree Gardens because they contained an ancient tree which had once been reputedly the meeting-place for the king's huntsmen, the General's pleasure-grounds included an open-air theatre as well as a bandstand and ample picnic facilities. How did the masses get there? The General's explanation shows that he was quick to recognise social innovations:

> Bicycling is an institution that must not be overlooked in any project for the improvement of the masses. The enormous distances bicyclists can go by road, especially on a Sunday, has rendered the population of country districts locomotive to an extent that has never been known before.

With an annual attendance of 16,839 at the Larmer Grounds in 1890, and 7000 at the museum – an interesting ratio – Pitt-Rivers had created a new sort of folk-festival, which Hardy wanted to see. In 1895 the General invited Hardy and Emma to stay at Rushmore at the climax of the year's programme in the Larmer Gardens – the annual sports-day which culminated in a concert and open-air dancing. The gardens were illuminated with thousands of Vauxhall lamps and for the last time in his life Hardy danced on the grass, having as his partner one of the General's daughters, Agnes Grove. It was a memorably romantic occasion, recalled vividly in old age when Hardy received news of Agnes's death, thirty years after their first encounter, and began to write the opening verses of the elegy entitled simply 'Concerning Agnes':

> I am stopped from hoping what I have hoped before –
> > Yes, many a time! –
> To dance with that fair woman yet once more
> > As in the prime
> Of August, when the wide-faced moon looked through
> The boughs at the faery lamps of the Larmer Avenue.

I could not, though I should wish, have over again
      That old romance,
And sit apart in the shade as we sat then
      After the dance
The while I held her hand, and, to the booms
Of contrabassos, feet still pulsed from the distant rooms.

Prominent among the great families of the Chase – along with the Pitts, Cecils, Herberts and Ashley Coopers – were the Arundells of Wardour Castle. The old castle has stood in ruins since its battering in the Civil War. The castle visited by Jude and Sue in *Jude the Obscure* was its replacement, built in 1770 on a new site: they discussed the two buildings, in terms that show Hardy's own architectural interest, when they were planning their day's outing from 'Melchester':

'Tomorrow is our grand day, you know. Where shall we go?'
'I have leave from three till nine. Wherever we can get to and come back from in that time. Not ruins, Jude – I don't care for them.'
'Well – Wardour Castle. And then we can do Fonthill if we like – all in the same afternoon.'
'Wardour is Gothic ruins – and I hate Gothic!'
'No. Quite otherwise. It is a classic building – Corinthian, I think; with a lot of pictures.'
'Ah – that will do. I like the sound of Corinthian. We'll go'.

To Wardour they went and spent some time wandering through the picture-galleries and commenting on the individual paintings that Hardy itemises. After the death of the last Earl of Arundell in 1944 this fine collection was gradually dispersed. The castle is now Cranborne Chase School.

Wardour is very close to the northern limit of the Chase, where it is bounded by the river Nadder. The general inclination of the Chase is to rise from south to north. It is in effect a chalk slope rearing away from the sandy heath of Egdon and a narrow band of clay near Cranborne which for centuries supported a pottery industry. The climbing emergence of the chalk brings a sudden change of character which culminates dramatically in Melbury Beacon, Win Green and the Ox Drove which runs along the escarpment above the Ebble valley; beyond the Ebble there is a second steep ridge which carried the old coach road up Whitesheet Hill to Salisbury; and finally the Chase dies away in the Vale of Wardour and the Nadder valley.

Win Green is the highest point in the Chase and — at 910 feet — one of the highest in southern England. The steeply rising and falling roads thereabouts were used by Alec d'Urberville to frighten Tess with his reckless driving, which threatened to overturn them. Win Green also figures in one of Hardy's odder poems 'The Vampirine Fair', in which the narrator tells how, in the absence overseas of her husband — Gilbert — she became the mistress of the lord of the manor and proceeded to ruin him:

> When Michaelmas browned the nether Coomb,
>   And Wingreen Hill above,
> And made the hollyhocks rags of bloom,
>   My lord grew ill of love.
>
> My lord grew ill with love for me;
>   Gilbert was far from port;
> And — so it was — that time did see
>   Me housed at Manor Court.

Win Green,
Cranborne Chase,
looking westward

The poem is worth noticing here as an example of the teasing puzzles that Hardy liked to scatter over Wessex, to be relished and discussed by his readers. The mention of Win Green adds a circumstantial air, which seems to hint that the story might be founded in truth, based perhaps on some legend in which 'the nether Coomb' and 'Manor Court' could be identified. There is a hamlet called 'Coombe' with a capital C on one side of Win Green; but then on the opposite side there is a combe known as 'Ashcombe', and Hardy's commentators have preferred Ashcombe – perhaps because it is near Rushmore, which is claimed to be 'Manor Court'. Historically, however, Rushmore was a keeper's lodge and hunting-box – never a manor courthouse. Berry Court on the Donhead side of Win Green might be a more plausible choice. At which point it is perhaps wise to conclude that this kind of enquiry is best pursued as a personal hobby, which enriches one's pleasure in the intimacies of the Wessex countryside without quite dispersing those mists of uncertainty that Hardy introduced into the atmosphere so cunningly.

The identification of 'Melchester' as Salisbury is a safer bet. In *Jude the Obscure* Hardy acclaimed the cathedral without reservation as 'the most graceful architectural pile in England'. His love of Salisbury was long-standing and constant, starting at the age of nineteen when he had his first sight of the cathedral during a visit to his sister Mary at the Training College, where she was studying to become a school-teacher – as the other sister, Kate, did later. In the writing of *Jude the Obscure* it must seem almost inevitable that Hardy should choose to locate the training of Sue Bridehead as a teacher in 'Melchester' at the 'ancient edifice of the fifteenth century, once a palace, now a training-school, with mullioned and transomed windows, and a courtyard in front shut in from the road by a wall' – which incidentally has ceased to be a training-college and is now the Salisbury and South Wilts Museum; and that Jude should work as a stone-mason on the Cathedral repairs, 'which were very extensive, the whole interior stonework having been overhauled, to be largely replaced by new'.

Over sixty years after that first visit Hardy paused on a journey through Salisbury for what was probably his last sight of the city. *The Life* records that 'they stopped for a little while to look at the Cathedral, as Hardy always loved doing, and at various old buildings, including the Training College which he had visited more than

165

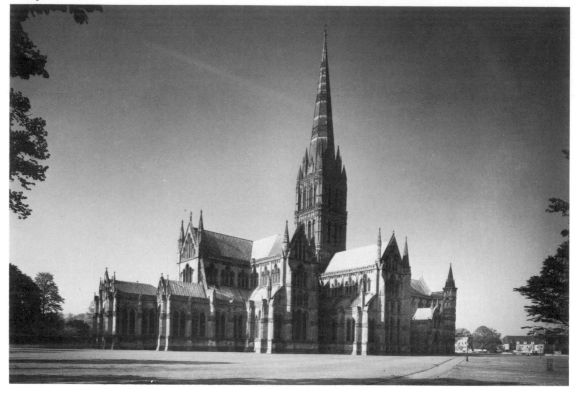

Salisbury Cathedral

fifty years before when his two sisters were students there, and which is faithfully described in *Jude the Obscure*'. Other aspects of Salisbury life appear in his writings – notably the amusement-fair in 'On the Western Circuit' with its steam roundabouts providing 'this most delightful holiday-game of our times'; but it is the cathedral which dominates the scene. Today as in Hardy's time it makes the most finished and telling affirmation of the Christian faith – with the silent impartiality of stone – to the devout, the doubter and the indifferent alike. It is a summation of a large part of the Wessex heritage which Hardy could neither accept totally nor reject totally.

The inner tension that it arouses shows in Sue's response when Jude suggests that they should go and sit in the cathedral:

> 'Cathedral? Yes. Though I think I'd rather sit in the railway station,' she answered, a remnant of vexation still in her voice. 'That's the centre of the town life now. The Cathedral has had its day!'

Two years after the publication of *Jude the Obscure* Hardy was again in Salisbury and was moved to write the poem 'A Cathedral Façade at Midnight'. *The Life* records, on 10 August 1897:

> Went into the Close late at night. The moon was visible through both the north and south clerestory windows to me standing on the turf on the north side ... Walked to the west front, and watched the moonlight creep round upon the statuary of the façade – stroking tentatively and then more and more firmly the prophets, the martyrs, the bishops, the kings, and the queens ... Upon the whole the Close of Salisbury, under the full summer moon on a windless midnight, is as beautiful a scene as any I know in England – or for the matter of that elsewhere.

The poem reflects this experience, opening with a description of the moonlight creeping 'along the sculptures of the western wall': its climax comes with

> sighings of regret
> At the ancient faith's rejection
> Under the sure, unhasting, steady stress
> Of Reason's movement, making meaningless
> The coded creeds of old-time godliness.

Yet *The Life* continues with an account of the afternoon service, at which Hardy and Emma were present and Hardy was deeply impressed by the first lesson (*Jeremiah VI*) – 'a beautiful chapter, beautifully read by the old Canon'. By his own account Hardy was 'churchy; not in an intellectual sense, but in so far as instincts and emotions ruled'. It was again Salisbury which inspired another poem exploring the anguish of a lost faith, 'The Impercipient', subtitled 'At a Cathedral Service', with its final poignant image of agnosticism –

> O, doth a bird deprived of wings
> Go earth-bound wilfully!

It is this complexity of thought and feeling which gives the Close the deeply involving atmosphere that gathers imperceptibly about all but the most insensitive of tourists. In the broad landscape of Hardy's Wessex nothing rears up more prominently – or with a more profound significance – than the tall spire of Salisbury.

167

In *A Shepherd's Life*, which is largely associated with Martin Down, W. H. Hudson emphasised another aspect of Salisbury:

> It is not of 'New Saresbyri' as seen by the tourist, with a mind full of history, archaeology, and the aesthetic delight in cathedrals, that I desire to write, but of Salisbury as it appears to the dweller on the Plain. For Salisbury is the capital of the Plain, the head and heart of all those villages, too many to count, scattered far and wide over the surrounding country. It is the villager's own peculiar City.

This is well said; Salisbury overlaps county boundaries to be something more than a county-town. It gathers together the valleys of the chalk streams, which are the arteries of the great expanse of downland that extends from Dorset to Hampshire and Berkshire. The Nadder, the Wylye, the Ebble, the Wiltshire Avon and the Bourne come together like fingers to be clenched in the hand of Salisbury. South of the city the Avon threads a sweet and fertile green through the dark heaths of Egdon and the New Forest. On every other side is the chalk, the rolling, extending, close-bitten, uncluttered line of the chalk.

Not everyone likes the chalk landscape. William Gilpin, the high-priest of the picturesque – parodied by William Combe as 'Doctor Syntax' – took the view that it 'spoils everything'. Thomas Huxley could see in it no more than 'a mutton-suggesting prettiness'. More sympathetic to the classic sheep-walks of southern England was Hudson, who proclaimed:

> Just as the air is purer and fresher on these chalk heights than on the earth below, and as the water is of a more crystal purity, and the sky perhaps bluer, so do all colours and all sounds have a purity and vividness and intensity beyond that of other places.

There is an undeniable monotony in the vistas of Salisbury Plain; and military occupation adds a distinctive blight. It is when the line of the chalk becomes sinuous and easily flowing into curves and folds that its beauty begins to show – in the northern scarp of the Vale of Pewsey, for instance, or such a characteristic downland village as Aldbourne. The general ambience of the downs is strongly represented in Hardy's stories – from Toller Down, where Gabriel Oak grazed his sheep, to the ploughland of 'Marygreen' (Fawley) where Jude was employed as a bird-scarer. On the Marlborough Downs the story 'What the Shepherd Saw' conjures up a traditional scene of 'a wheeled hut of the kind commonly in use among sheep-keepers during the early lambing season' standing within sight of 'a Druidical trilithon, consisting of three oblong stones in the form of a doorway, two on end and one across as a lintel'.

It is these conspicuous remains of our earliest civilisations which give an added interest to the chalk downs and particularly to the Wiltshire downs. Silbury Hill, the West Kennett long barrow, Avebury, the Wansdyke — these are some of the classic items of British archaeology; and supreme among them, of course, is Stonehenge, to which Hardy was drawn as the fitting scene for the conclusion of Tess's flight with Angel after the killing of Alec d'Urberville. There she could be seen to act out again some profound ritual of sacrifice and expiation, echoing that earlier cry of hers, 'Once victim, always victim — that's the law!'

At the first light of daybreak, when the black cloud of night began to lift bodily 'like the lid of a pot, letting in at the earth's edge the coming day', Angel kept vigil while Tess slept briefly; and by degrees the setting of Stonehenge became visible:

> The band of silver paleness along the east horizon made even the distant parts of the Great Plain appear dark and near; and the whole enormous landscape bore that impress of reserve, taciturnity, and hesitation which is usual just before day. The eastward pillars and their architraves stood up blackly against the light, and the great flame-shaped Sun-stone beyond them; and the Stone of Sacrifice midway. Presently the night wind died out, and the quivering little pools in the cup-like hollows of the stones lay still.

In his final novel Hardy moved further eastwards to the Berkshire Downs, between Hungerford and Wantage. In *Jude the Obscure* it was clearly a tribute to the grandmother who had quickened his boyish imagination that lay behind Hardy's choice of the names of Jude Fawley and 'Marygreen'. The grandmother's name was Mary and her childhood had been spent at Fawley, on which 'Marygreen' is based.

There are two Fawleys to the south of Oxford, the other being near Henley: the need to distinguish them may account for the prefix Great before the one Hardy had in mind, since its claim to greatness would otherwise be difficult to support. In the novel it is referred to as a 'little village, or rather hamlet' and Hardy's description continues:

> It was as old-fashioned as it was small, and it rested in the lap of an undulating upland adjoining the North Wessex downs. Old as it was, however, the well-shaft was probably the only relic of the local history that remained absolutely unchanged. Many of the thatched and dormered dwelling-houses had been pulled down of late years, and many trees felled on the green. Above all, the original church, hump-backed, wood-turreted, and quaintly hipped, had been taken down, and either cracked up into heaps of road-metal in the lane, or utilized as pig-sty walls, garden-seats, guard-stones to fences, and rockeries in the flower-beds of the neighbourhood. In place of it a tall new building of modern Gothic design, unfamiliar to English eyes, had been erected on a new piece of ground by a certain obliterator of historic records who had run down from London and back in a day.

The radical 'restoration' or demolition and rebuilding of ancient churches, in which as a young man he had himself been regretfully involved, was a subject that engaged Hardy's feelings increasingly in his later years. The architect of the new church at Fawley, dismissed so scornfully by Hardy, was G.E. Street, whose best-known work is the London Law Courts. Fawley church, with its apse and its Burne-Jones window, is indeed 'unfamiliar' in the context of a Wessex village but it has its admirers and its champions – John Betjeman among them. Its foreignness is mediated moreover by at least one homely touch: the receptacle provided for the receipt of offerings bears the words 'Beef Dripping'.

What gives Fawley its air of prosperity today is its stud farm. This is race-horse country, with a well-known racing stable at nearby Whatcombe. The gallops on Woolley Down have seen the training of three Derby winners, including the famous Blenheim, and the area is best understood as a part of the Lambourn Downs. Here we reach what is effectively the north-eastern limit of the Wessex downland. To go any further is to descend into either the Vale of the White Horse or the valley of the Thames. The two cities whose presences now begin to be felt are Oxford and Reading: as

On Walton Hill looking westwards to Sedgemoor

The Dorset coast, near Chideock

Above: *The Vale of Avalon and Glastonbury Tor*

Right: *Cranborne Chase: a hurdle-maker near Ashmore*

Left: *Salisbury Cathedral and the river Avon*

Below: *Pilsdon Pen, near Broadwindsor*

Right: *Exmoor: Dunkery Beacon*

Below: *The village of Abbotsbury*

Weymouth: the Esplanade

Right: *Bere Regis church: the Turberville window*

Below: *The Larmer Tree Gardens, Tollard Royal*

Above: *The Roman road from Badbury Rings to Old Sarum*

Left: *The entrance to Boscastle harbour*

Bournemouth: pine trees in Branksome Chine

'Christminster' and 'Aldbrickham' they have prominent roles in the story of *Jude*, but so does London in *The Hand of Ethelberta*. They seem to me to lie outside the bounds of what is felt to be Hardy country. When the boy Jude made his first venture to the east-west ridgeway that runs north of Fawley he was at a frontier where 'the white road seemed to ascend and diminish till it joined the sky'. Over the ridge lay another world:

> Till now he had had no suspicion that such a wide, flat low-lying country lay so near at hand, under the very verge of his upland world. The whole northern semi-circle between east and west, to a distance of forty or fifty miles, spread itself before him; a bluer, moister atmosphere, evidently, than that he breathed up here.

To this position the boy returned, in his desire to see distant Christminster; to be rewarded, when he climbed a ladder leaning against an old barn known as the Brown House, with the sight of points of light in the gathering dusk as the rays of the setting sun touched the city's 'vanes, windows, wet roof slates, and other shining spots upon the spires, domes, freestone-work, and varied outlines that were faintly revealed. It was Christminster, unquestionably; either directly seen, or miraged in the peculiar atmosphere'.

The Brown House has disappeared. The view has had added to it the cooling towers of Didcot power-station, but it remains an impressive panorama even if the familiar haze conceals any glimpse of Oxford.

CHAPTER TEN

Wessex Heights

There are some heights in Wessex, shaped as if by a kindly hand
For thinking, dreaming, dying on, and at crises when I stand,
Say, on Ingpen Beacon eastward, or on Wylls-Neck westwardly,
I seem where I was before my birth, and after death may be.

In what might understandably be claimed as his finest poem,
'Wessex Heights', Hardy revealed the ultimate fastness of Wessex
into which his spirit could retreat from the cares and stresses and
failures of life as they oppressed him 'down there' in the arenas of
every day. It carried the tones of a middle-aged man separating
himself from the prime heat of life: it was written in 1896, when he
could look back on a quarter of a century as a hard-working novelist
whose career he had now terminated, and when his passionate
nature had come to admit that 'Time cures hearts of tenderness'. It
is in this mood of valedictory weariness that he echoes the words
of the Psalmist – 'I will lift up mine eyes unto the hills from whence
cometh my help'.

The heights of Wessex are a recurring theme in Hardy's writings
– High Stoy, Bubb Down, 'homely Bulbarrow', Nettlecombe Tout,
'little Pilsdon Crest' and many more form a sort of litany of praise.
Although none of them reaches the senior altitude of a thousand
feet, which must be every hill's ambition, they are nevertheless one
of the definitive elements in the whole character of Wessex – indeed
one of its glories. The dramatic cliffs and promontories of the Dorset
coast, from Hengistbury Head to Golden Cap, find an answering
echo inland in the range of heights that extends from Win Green to
Toller Down and Pilsdon Pen. What they may lack in inches is
compensated by steepness of gradient which makes them rear up in

a majestically commanding manner above the vales and combes at their feet. There is no denying the sheer exhilaration of the spirit that comes to anyone who stands on Bulbarrow looking across Blackmore Vale and Somerset to Glastonbury Tor and the Mendips; or on Win Green looking south over Cranborne Chase to the Needles, and northwards to Salisbury Plain. These are visionary moments – in Wordsworth's phrase 'felt in the blood, and felt along the heart'. For Hardy the heights of Wessex were a final citadel, a place of retreat

Where men have never cared to haunt nor women have walked
        with me,
And ghosts then keep their distance; and I know some liberty.

The western moors of Devon and Cornwall lie outside this grouping. Hardy extends the range to Inkpen Beacon on the Hampshire-Berkshire border and to Wylls Neck on the Quantocks as his limits.

Evening light from Bulbarrow

Inkpen or Ingpen fits harmoniously into the general downland scene: its hogsback perch faces the Lambourn Downs northwards. Wylls Neck seems a more capricious choice, for Hardy had very little association personally with the Quantocks. As is so often the case with him, the broader Wessex gesture tends to conceal the fact that the deeper intensity of his feeling gathers about the Dorset element. In the novels it is the north Dorset escarpment overlooking Blackmore Vale which constantly recurs.

The most detailed single portrayal, however, is a little further west: Toller Down with its associated hill, 'Norcombe', figures prominently in *Far from the Madding Crowd*, and in the poem 'The Homecoming'. The lonely desolate character of Toller Down is well established in the poem, which is a gently satirical account of a young bride's dismay on first arrival at her husband's grim home-stead, with its 'great black beams for ceiling, and floor o' wretched stone'. While she pines and wishes to be 'home again with dear daddee!' Hardy introduces each verse with a couplet reflecting the inhospitable darkness outside:

Gruffly growled the wind on Toller downland broad and bare,
And lonesome was the house, and dark; and few came there.

In *Far from the Madding Crowd* 'Norcombe Hill' is described as 'not far from lonely Toller-Down', and it is tempting to take 'Norcombe' as a Hardyesque *alias* for Westcombe, which is close to Toller Whelme. It was on Norcombe Hill that Gabriel Oak grazed his flock of sheep in the general vicinity of Toller Down, and the night scene at the commencement of the story is one of Hardy's most elaborate and imaginative portrayals of a Wessex landscape – so elaborately detailed indeed that I have felt obliged to abridge it:

It was nearly midnight on the eve of St Thomas's, the shortest day in the year. A desolating wind wandered from the north over the hill, which was covered on its northern side by an ancient and decaying plantation of beeches. Tonight these trees sheltered the southern slope from the keenest blasts, which smote the wood and floundered through it with a sound as of grumbling, or gushed over its crowning boughs in a weakened moan. The dry leaves in the ditch simmered and boiled in the same breezes, a tongue of air occasionally ferreting out a few, and sending them spinning across the grass.

The instinctive act of humankind was to stand and listen, and learn how the trees on the right and the trees on the left wailed or chaunted to each other in the regular antiphonies of a cathedral choir; how hedges and other shapes to leeward then caught the note, lowering it to the tenderest sob; and how the hurrying gust then plunged into the south, to be heard no more.

The sky was clear — remarkably clear — and the twinkling of all the stars seemed to be but throbs of one body, timed by a common pulse. A difference of colour in the stars — oftener read of than seen in England — was really perceptible here. The sovereign brilliancy of Sirius pierced the eye with a steely glitter, the star called Capella was yellow, Aldebaran and Betelgueux shone with a fiery red.

To persons standing alone on a hill during a clear midnight such as this, the roll of the world eastward is almost a palpable movement.

In its serial form in the *Cornhill* magazine this appeared anonymously, leading an admiring reviewer in the *Spectator* to guess that the author might be George Eliot — a speculation which so amused and delighted the editor of the *Cornhill*, Leslie Stephen, that he wrote to Hardy: 'The gentle *Spectator* thinks you must be George Eliot because you know the names of the stars'.

There is one thing more to be said about Norcombe Hill. It demonstrates most clearly the way these 'partly real, partly dream' landscapes of Wessex are enmeshed with the men and women who move among them. The character of Gabriel Oak is embodied in Hardy's vision of Norcombe Hill. As we are drawn into that graphic midnight scene we enter also into the deeper atmosphere of the story and the forces that will bear on the drama that begins to unfold:

Norcombe Hill — not far from lonely Toller Down — was one of the spots which suggest to a passerby that he is in the presence of a shape approaching the indestructible as nearly as any to be found on earth. It was a featureless convexity of chalk and soil — an ordinary specimen of those smoothly-outlined protuberances of the globe which may remain undisturbed on some great day of confusion, when far grander heights and dizzy granite precipices topple down.

'Featureless' and 'ordinary' – these are the concealing attributes of that staunch survivor, Gabriel Oak, who is described as occupying 'morally the vast middle space of Laodicean neutrality' and as 'a man whose moral colour was a kind of pepper-and-salt mixture'. He embodies the unspectacular, undemonstrative virtues that Hardy liked to display in his Wessex heroes, in contrast with the impetuous passions and wayward impulses of Gabriel's rivals – Sergeant Troy and Mr Boldwood. It is Troy and Boldwood who are represented in the grander heights and dizzy precipices which will eventually topple down, while Oak persists as a virtually indestructible Norcombe Hill among the Alps of treachery and the Himalayas of hatred.

These landscapes of Hardy's are not idly pretty sequences of fine writing but theatres of his imagination in which character and background reinforce each other. They answer to the comment he made on Turner's water-colours – 'each is a landscape *plus* a man's soul'. On another occasion he wrote: 'The "simply natural" is interesting no longer. The much decried, mad, late-Turner rendering is now necessary to create my interest. The exact truth as to material fact ceases to be of importance in art'. And he proclaimed his own desire 'to see the deeper reality underlying the scenic'.

It is in that mood that he describes the wintry hostility of the uplands when Tess goes to work at Flintcomb-Ash. It is a place denied the panoramic amplitude of the Heights, being set back a few miles to the south of Nettlecombe Tout and Church Hill. Where the Valley of the Great Dairies had been a lush and bounteous scene in the heat of summer, Flintcomb-Ash is 'a starve-acre place': the stirring sexuality of the weeks with Angel at Talbothays is mocked now by the phallic shapes of the flints that Marian picks up as a coarse jest. And as the winter deepens it approaches such a severity as has not been known for years:

> Amid this scene Tess slaved in the morning frosts and in the afternoon rains. When it was not swede-grubbing it was swede-trimming, in which process they sliced off the earth and the fibres with a bill-hook before storing the roots for future use. At this occupation they could shelter themselves by a thatched hurdle if it rained; but if it was frosty even their thick leather gloves could not prevent the frozen masses they handled from biting their fingers.

To emphasise the starkness of the scene Hardy introduced some sinister birds which appeared as the only companions of the girls as they worked in the fields:

> After this season of congealed dampness came a spell of dry frost, when strange birds from behind the North Pole began to arrive silently on the upland of Flintcomb-Ash; gaunt spectral creatures with tragical eyes — eyes which had witnessed scenes of cataclysmal horror in inaccessible polar regions of a magnitude such as no human being had ever conceived, in curdling temperatures that no man could endure; which had beheld the crash of icebergs and the slide of snow-hills by the shooting light of the Aurora; been half blinded by the whirl of colossal storms and terraqueous distortions; and retained the expression of feature that such scenes had engendered.

The nature and origin of these remarkable birds are somewhat unexpected. They are ducks and they come from the pages of *The Return of the Native*, where Diggory Venn feels himself to be in direct communication with regions unknown to men when he comes upon a mallard — 'just arrived from the home of the north wind. The creature brought within him an amplitude of Northern knowledge. Glacial catastrophes, snowstorm episodes, glittering auroral effects, Polaris in the zenith, Franklin underfoot — the category of his commonplaces was wonderful'.

The duck is of all birds the one least suited to suggest horror and menace so Hardy wisely refrained from naming the birds of Flintcomb-Ash. It was the thought of Arctic migration that suggested the atmosphere he wanted to create. It is true that the arable uplands of north Dorset will seldom receive winter visitors more exotic than fieldfares and plovers; but if the 'gaunt spectral creatures' that Tess saw are not to be found in today's ornithological field-guides they are safe enough in that special zoo of the poets, where such endangered species as the unicorn and the basilisk survive.

The undertow of hostility and weirdness extended from Flintcomb-Ash to other features of the uplands. In her abortive walk to Angel's home at 'Emminster' (Beaminster) Tess passed, on Batcombe Hill, the stone pillar known as Cross-in-Hand, marking 'the site of a miracle, or murder, or both'. The legend of the miracle,

Batcombe Hill

involving a priest from Cerne Abbey, was versified by Hardy in 'The Lost Pyx'. The general scene was described more fully in *Tess*:

Of all spots on the bleached and desolate upland this was the most forlorn. It was so far removed from the charm which is sought in landscape by artists and view-lovers as to reach a new kind of beauty, a negative beauty of tragic tone. The place took its name from a stone pillar which stood there, a strange rude monolith, from a stratum unknown in any local quarry, on which was roughly carved a human hand. Differing accounts were given of its history and purport. Some authorities stated that a devotional cross had once formed the complete erection thereon, of which the present relic was but the stump; others that the stone as it stood was entire, and that it had been fixed there to mark a boundary or place of meeting. Anyhow, whatever the origin of the relic, there was and is something sinister, or solemn, according to mood, in the scene amid which it stands; something tending to impress the most phlegmatic passer-by.

No less likely to impress the most phlegmatic passer-by is the Cerne Giant. This too is the subject of various legends, such as the one – noted by Hardy – that the men of Cerne Abbas have no whiskers. He also recorded the belief that a living giant, who used to eat a sheep a day, threatened to descend on Cerne on a particular night when he would ravish all the young women, and next day kill all the young men: in desperation the people of Cerne waylaid the Giant, killed him and cut his effigy on the hill-side.

A variant of this occurs in *The Dynasts* during the scene on Rainbarrows' Beacon when the Cantles and others are discussing an atrocious rumour about Napoleon that nobody likes to speak plainly, until Mrs Cantle says, 'I can tell you a word or two on't. It is about His victuals. They say that He lives upon human flesh, and has rashers of baby every morning for breakfast – for all the world like the Cernel Giant in old ancient times!'

The Giant of Cerne is now faithfully and clearly outlined in all his rude virility, but in the early years of this century he was so neglected and overgrown with grass as to be nearly invisible. The village also, according to Treves, was empty and decaying. 'Grass is growing in the streets,' he wrote, 'many houses have been long deserted, many have their windows boarded up, or are falling into listless ruin'. His words are a reminder of the workings of change in Hardy's Wessex. The railway's displacement of the horse-drawn coach was one revolutionary factor; another was the struggle in agriculture to come to terms with steam-power and with cheap imports from the new lands of America and Australasia.

Tess's experiences at Flintcomb-Ash point up most sharply the changing agricultural scene that Hardy had touched on earlier – in the Egdon Heath 'improvers', for example, in *The Return of the Native*. The pastoral landscapes of the dairying districts might be tranquil enough in their traditional ways but the arable of the upland chalk had been invaded by the steam-plough and the threshing-machine – that 'red tyrant' which made such despotic demands on the endurance of Tess's muscles and nerves.

179

In the poem he wrote in honour of the jubilee of the *Cornhill* magazine in 1910 Hardy contemplated the traditional rural scene on the *Cornhill*'s cover and contrasted it with the reality of new methods:

> — Here, on your cover, never tires
> The sower, reaper, thresher, while
> As through the seasons of our sires
>
> Each wills to work in ancient style
> With seedlip, sickle, share and flail,
> Though modes have since moved many a mile!
>
> The steel-roped plough now rips the vale,
> With cog and tooth the sheaves are won,
> Wired wheels drum out the wheat like hail.

The mechanical reaper-and-binder was still horse-drawn but the steam-plough and the threshing-machine brought a new man on to the farming landscape — the engineer. He was in Hardy's eyes an alien figure:

> He was in the agricultural world, but not of it. He served fire and smoke; these denizens of the fields served vegetation, weather, frost and sun. He travelled with his engine from farm to farm, from county to county, for as yet the steam threshing-machine was itinerant in this part of Wessex. He spoke in a strange northern accent; his thoughts being turned inwards upon himself, his eye on his iron charge, hardly perceiving the scenes around him, and caring for them not at all: holding only strictly necessary intercourse with the natives, as if some ancient doom compelled him to wander here against his will in the service of his Plutonic master. The long strap which ran from the driving-wheel of his engine to the red thresher under the rick was the sole tie-line between agriculture and him.

In the last quarter of the nineteenth century there was a growing anxiety at the transformation of the rural scene by scientific improvers, and a haunting nostalgia for the old traditional ways; while at the same time there was a recognition that the march of 'Progress' could not be halted for romantic reasons. Richard Jefferies, like Hardy, was caught in this conflict between reason and sentiment.

In *Hodge and his Masters*, which Jefferies published in 1880, the spokesman for Progress puts forward his views in these terms:

> Nothing will ever convince me that it was intended for English agriculturists to go on using wooden ploughs, to wear smock-frocks, and plod round and round in the same old track for ever. In no other way but by science, by steam, by machinery, by artificial manure, and, in one word, by the exercise of intelligence, can we compete with the world.

It is the voice of Jefferies himself, in one mood; but in another he writes: 'Here in the heart of the meadows romance has departed. Everything is mechanical or scientific'. Hardy reflects the same dilemma. In his essay 'The Dorsetshire Labourer' he puts a different complexion on the fieldwomen of Flintcomb-Ash and their kind:

> The women have, in many districts, acquired the rollicking air of factory hands. That seclusion and immutability, which was so bad for their pockets, was an unrivalled fosterer of their personal charm in the eyes of those whose experiences had been less limited. But the artistic merit of their old condition is scarcely a reason why they should have continued in it when other communities were marching on so vigorously towards uniformity and mental equality. It is only the old story that progress and picturesqueness do not harmonize. They are losing their individuality, but they are widening the range of their ideas, and gaining in freedom. It is too much to expect them to remain stagnant and old-fashioned for the pleasure of romantic spectators.

Before the introduction of artificial manures it was the sheep which was, in one farmer's phrase, 'the dung-cart of the downs'. Among the archetypal figures that Hardy set in his Wessex landscape Gabriel Oak the Shepherd ranks with Tess the Dairymaid. What made the downland scene as Hardy knew it was the association of shepherd and hurdle-maker. The closely cropped unbroken sward of the downland and the coppiced hazel from which hurdles are made — these were the dominant elements in much of the countryside. Today they have become increasingly rare. Neglected coppices are sometimes tolerated as cover for pheasants, and sometimes grubbed out. Old downland turf, rich in orchids and

Fontmell Down

many other wild-flowers, needs to be on a steep gradient if it is to escape the plough indefinitely.

The shepherd was for centuries the kingpin among the farm-workers of Wessex. John Aubrey in the seventeenth century described the shepherds of Wiltshire in their traditional garb of 'a long white cloak with a very deep cape, which comes halfway down their backs, made of the locks of the sheep'. They carried 'a sheep-crooke, a sling, a scrip, their tar-box, and a pipe or flute'. Defoe, journeying from Shaftesbury to Salisbury along the heights of Cran-borne Chase, was afraid he might lose his way as there was neither house nor town in view, but was able to record gratefully:

There is a certain never failing assistance upon all these downs for telling a stranger his way, and that is the number of shepherds feeding, or keeping their vast flocks of sheep, which are everywhere in the way, and who, with a very little pains, a traveller may always speak with. Nothing can be like it, the Arcadians' plains of which we read so much pastoral trumpery in the poets, could be nothing to them.

This long tradition flourished still in Hardy's lifetime. In 1897, to take an example close to the date of *Tess*, the sheep fair at Wilton attracted nearly eleven and a half thousand ewes and lambs. Despite his anxiety, after the success of *Far from the Madding Crowd*, to show that he could write about other subjects than shepherds and sheepfolds, Hardy gave a due regard to what was so integral a part of Wessex life. The opening scene of *The Mayor of Casterbridge* is set at 'Weydon Priors' (Weyhill) during the Fair 'where many hundreds of horses and sheep had been exhibited and sold in the forenoon'. Weyhill was an important fair, but twenty years later 'the real business of the fair had considerably dwindled. The new periodical great markets of neighbouring towns were beginning to interfere seriously with the trade carried on here for centuries. The pens for sheep, the tie-ropes for horses, were about half as long as they had been'.

Pummery Fair, on the outskirts of Dorchester, was perhaps the sort of urban market that was drawing away trade from the older fairs. It comes to life vividly in the poem 'A Sheep Fair':

> The day arrives of the autumn fair,
>   And torrents fall,
> Though sheep in throngs are gathered there,
>   Ten thousand all,
> Sodden, with hurdles round them reared:
> And, lot by lot, the pens are cleared,
> And the auctioneer wrings out his beard,
> And wipes his book, bedrenched and smeared,
> And rakes the rain from his face with the edge of his hand,
>   As torrents fall.
>
> The wool of the ewes is like a sponge
>   With the daylong rain:
> Jammed tight, to turn, or lie, or lunge,
>   They strive in vain.
> Their horns are soft as finger-nails,
> Their shepherds reek against the rails,
> The tied dogs soak with tucked-in tails,
> The buyers' hat-brims fill like pails,
> Which spill small cascades when they shift their stand
>   In the daylong rain.

It is the fair at 'the decayed old town of Kingsbere' (Bere Regis) which preserves most completely the atmosphere and detail of these great occasions in the farming year of Victorian Wessex. The fair was located on Woodbury Hill, outside the little town; Hardy visited it in 1873, so his portrayal of it as 'Greenhill' Fair in *Far from the Madding Crowd* is at first hand and immediate:

Greenhill was the Nijni Novgorod of South Wessex; and the busiest, merriest, noisiest day of the whole statute number was the day of the sheep fair. This yearly gathering was upon the summit of a hill which retained in good preservation the remains of an ancient earthwork, consisting of a huge rampart and entrenchment of an oval form encircling the top of the hill, though somewhat broken down here and there. To each of the two chief openings on opposite sides a winding road ascended, and the level green space of ten or fifteen acres enclosed by the bank was the site of the fair.

Thither in slow procession came the sheep, 'multitude after multitude, horned and hornless'. Hardy described the different breeds – South Downs and Dorset horned; Oxfordshires, Leicesters and Cotswolds; even a small flock of Exmoors. Some came from local farms, others from afar:

Shepherds who attended with their flocks from long distances started from home two or three days, or even a week, before the fair, driving their charges a few miles each day – not more than ten or twelve – and resting them at night in hired fields by the wayside at previously chosen points, where they fed, having fasted since morning. The shepherd of each flock marched behind, a bundle containing his kit for the week strapped upon his shoulders, and in his hand his crook, which he used as the staff of his pilgrimage.

Greenhill and Pummery belong to the southern slope of the downland, where the chalk begins to dip towards the sand of Egdon Heath and the alluvial valley of the Great Dairies. The heights, from Bulbarrow to Bubb Down, are a watershed sending tributaries northwards to join the Stour in Blackmore Vale, while they water the southern slopes with the Piddle, the Cerne, the Frome, the Bere and many lesser streams which find their way eventually into the

Frome or the Piddle. Of the southern river settlements along the margin of the central chalk plateau the ones which stand out conspicuously are a notable trio — the three which Hardy names 'Weatherbury' (Puddletown), 'Kingsbere' (Bere Regis) and 'Casterbridge' (Dorchester).

The river Piddle is of rather more account than its name might suggest. Rising near Alton Pancras it cuts a narrow valley through the chalk uplands, running roughly parallel to the river Cerne and linking together a number of villages that bear its name — Piddletrenthide, Piddlehinton, Puddletown, Tolpuddle, Affpuddle, Briantspuddle and Turners Puddle. Piddle and Puddle are optional variants, to which Hardy ingeniously added 'Pydel' in the poem 'A Sunday Morning Tragedy'. Among the Piddle villages Tolpuddle claims attention for its Martyrs, Affpuddle for its tranquil grouping of church, mill and cottages: the whole valley is full of echoes of Hardy stories and poems, and nowhere more so than in Puddletown.

As a young man Hardy's grandfather had played the cello in Puddletown church, before he began married life at Bockhampton; and it is this church, with its musicians' gallery intact, which now evokes the bygone world of the little bands of church musicians whom Hardy portrayed in *Under the Greenwood Tree*. The intense dedication to music — both sacred and profane — of the three generations of Hardys was a civilising and inspirational factor in the development of the future novelist and poet. Grandfather Hardy reformed the music in Stinsford church when he settled at Bockhampton but he continued to play his cello in other churches in the neighbourhood. His two sons played with him, as they grew old enough to do so. At Stinsford the 'Mellstock Quire' was limited to strings — usually four. Puddletown, so Hardy tells us in *The Life*, could boast of eight players but these 'included wood wind and leather — that is to say, clarionets and serpents — which were apt to be a little too sonorous, even strident, when zealously blown'.

Besides playing in church and at barn-dances the village musicians were an essential part of wedding processions, like the one in *The Woodlanders* when Timothy Tangs and his bride Suke Damson, with their friends 'be just walking round the parishes to show ourselves a bit'. There were many Hardy relatives in Puddletown and the 'Mellstock' musicians must often have lent

185

their services to such an occasion as the poem 'The Country Wedding' describes:

> Little fogs were gathered in every hollow,
> But the purple hillocks enjoyed fine weather
> As we marched with our fiddles over the heather
> — How it comes back! — to their wedding that day.
>
> Our getting there brought our neighbours and all, O!
> Till, two and two, the couples stood ready.
> And her father said: 'Souls, for God's sake, be steady!'
> And we strung up our fiddles, and sounded out 'A'.
>
> The groomsman he stared, and said, 'You must follow!'
> But we'd gone to fiddle in front of the party,
> (Our feelings as friends being true and hearty)
> And fiddle in front we did — all the way.
>
> Yes, from their door by Mill-tail-Shallow,
> And up Styles-Lane, and by Front-Street houses,
> Where stood maids, bachelors, and spouses,
> Who cheered the songs that we knew how to play.
>
> I bowed the treble before her father,
> Michael the tenor in front of the lady,
> The bass-viol Reub — and right well played he! —
> The serpent Jim; ay, to church and back.

At Bere Regis ('Kingsbere') as at Puddletown it is the church which claims attention. Where Puddletown has its musicians' gallery, Bere Regis can show with equal pride its d'Urberville window. Before the Dissolution the church at Bere Regis belonged in part to the nuns of Tarrant Crawford and in part to the d'Urberville family. The celebrated window displays the various heraldic quarterings of the arms of the d'Urbervilles in what might be described as a genealogy without words. It is easy to imagine its effect on Hardy, who was very conscious of 'the decline and fall of the Hardys'. In his youth his mother had pointed out a man walking beside a horse and common spring-trap as the representative of 'what was once the leading branch of the family'. And Hardy commented 'So we go down, down, down.'

Bere Regis Church

The fruit of that experience was the character of Jack Dur-beyfield, the poor deluded father of Tess who fancied himself to be Sir John d'Urberville with hundreds of ancestors lying in vaults under Kingsbere church 'in coats of mail and jewels, in gr't lead coffins weighing tons and tons' – a thought which convinces him that 'there's not a man in the county o' South-Wessex that's got grander and nobler skillentons in his family than I'. When, after his death, the family is evicted they go to Kingsbere and camp temporarily over the vaults, with Mrs Durbeyfield claiming hopefully that 'your family vault is your own freehold'.

At times Hardy liked to satirise 'that touching faith in members of long-established families as such, irrespective of their personal condition or character, which is still found among old-fashioned people in the rural districts'; and his version of Miller Loveday's pedigree in *The Trumpet-Major* is a delicious parody. Nevertheless he used more than once the saying he put into Mrs Durbeyfield's mouth – 'Tis well to be kin to a coach, even if you don't ride in 'en'. The social power and influence of the great dynastic families of Wessex were very considerable in Hardy's lifetime and are not inconsiderable today.

Dorchester ('Casterbridge') I have kept till last. Of all the towns of Wessex it is the one most deeply impregnated with Hardy's own personality and with scenes and characters and perceptions of many sorts in his writings. At the County Museum the collection of manuscripts and Hardyana attracts scholars from all over the world. The County Reference Library holds a second collection of growing importance. His statue, sculpted by Eric Kennington, is a local landmark, near the library. The house he built here, Max Gate, is well cared for as a private residence. Like any other substantial English town Dorchester has been greatly modified to suit the new ways of the twentieth century, but it retains much of the old-fashioned market-town atmosphere that Hardy captured in *The Mayor of Casterbridge*. In that novel Elizabeth-Jane was struck by the fact that the town was all huddled together – 'shut in by a square wall of trees, like a plot of garden ground by a box-edging'; and Hardy likened it, in its compactness, to a box of dominoes:

There was no suburb in the modern sense, or transitional intermixture of town and down. It stood, with regard to the wide

*Statue of Thomas
Hardy, Dorchester*

fertile land adjoining, clean-cut and distinct, like a chess-board
on a green table-cloth. The farmer's boy could sit under his
barley-mow and pitch a stone into the office-window of the
town-clerk; reapers at work among the sheaves nodded to ac-
quaintances standing on the pavement-corner; the red-robed
judge, when he condemned a sheep-stealer, pronounced sentence
to the tune of Baa, that floated in at the window from the remainder of the flock browsing hard by; and at executions the waiting
crowd stood in a meadow immediately before the drop, out of
which the cows had been temporarily driven to give spectators
room.

The decision to settle permanently in Dorchester was recorded in
The Life in a distinctly grudging spirit, as 'a step they often
regretted having taken'. Hardy was at pains to emphasise that the
town was to be their 'country-quarters', several months of each
year being spent in London, with occasional spells abroad. He obviously needed forms of intellectual stimulus that Dorchester could

189

Sherborne Abbey

not provide. Its nearest comparable inland neighbours, Sherborne and Salisbury, have a bolder and more sophisticated style – if only from the presence of abbey, castle and cathedral: they seem to draw together more numerous strands of life, where Casterbridge enshrines a narrowly agricultural tradition, as Hardy described it:

Casterbridge lived by agriculture at one remove further from the fountain head than the adjoining villages – no more. The townsfolk understood every fluctuation in the rustic's condition, for it affected their receipts as much as the labourer's; they entered into the troubles and joys which moved the aristocratic families ten miles round – for the same reason. And even at the dinner-parties of the professional families the subjects of discussion were corn, cattle-disease, sowing and reaping, fencing and planting.

Outside the farming interest were the barracks and the gaol. There is no mistaking the blend of glamorous danger and suppressed violence which the countryfolk found in the town's atmosphere. In the complex chemistry of Hardy's imagination Dorchester's public hangings and whippings were ingredients of some consequence: so too were the young soldiers in their smart uniforms, and the girls they left behind them.

> Now Jenny's life had hardly been
> A life of modesty;
> And few in Casterbridge had seen
> More loves of sorts than she
> From scarcely sixteen years above;
> Among them sundry troopers of
> The King's-Own Cavalry.

That is a verse from 'The Dance at the Phoenix', which contains so much of the raw vitality of Dorchester and portrays its urban scene in faithful detail, before its tenderly ironical conclusion:

> Well! times are not as times were then,
> Nor fair ones half so free;
> And truly they were martial men,
> The King's-Own Cavalry,
> And when they went from Casterbridge
> And vanished over Mellstock Ridge,
> 'Twas saddest morn to see.

Dorchester is no longer a garrison town; Jack Ketch with his whips and the hangman with his noose come there no more; there are no girls sitting on Grey's Bridge and singing 'Take me, Paddy, will you now?' The town has become the administrative centre for a county much bigger in area and more numerous in population than Michael Henchard and his contemporaries could have foreseen. To lord it over Poole and Bournemouth is a strange destiny for this slow-moving, old-fashioned place which does not have the buildings, the institutions, the sheer 'presence' for such a task.

191

Yet there is something, less easily defined, still to be mentioned: it is the stir and murmur of Casterbridge voices that rise through Hardy's poetry and prose with an unforgettable humanity of tone and feeling. In some towns and cities the inhabitants seem to be dwarfed by the majesty of the buildings or the richness of the place's history or some other powerful factor. Dorchester has its Roman heritage but the town is frankly undistinguished – a cheerful jumble of this and that. The 'Casterbridge' to be found in Dorchester today is not so much in brick and stone as in face and voice – the echoes and the memories of the many thumb-nail sketches Hardy made. To recall them is to be embarrassed by the wealth there is to choose from, and to be overwhelmed by the poignancy of phrase and feeling that so often lights up what might have been commonplace. I think of Mother Cuxsom's catalogue of the little housewifely indignities that Susan Henchard must suffer in death – 'All her shining keys will be took from her, and her cupboards opened; and little things 'a didn't wish seen, anybody will see; and her wishes and ways will all be as nothing!'

It is this combination of humble living and strong feeling which colours Hardy's portrayal of the chance encounters and overheard remarks in the streets of Casterbridge, bringing before us such an unexpected character as Patty Beech:

> And are ye one of Hermitage –
> Of Hermitage, by Ivel Road,
> And do ye know, in Hermitage
> A thatch-roofed house where sengreens grow?
> And does John Waywood live there still –
> He of the name that there abode
> When father hurdled on the hill
>   Some fifteen years ago?
>
> Does he now speak o' Patty Beech,
> The Patty Beech he used to – see,
> Or ask at all if Patty Beech
> Is known or heard of out this way?
> – Ask ever if she's living yet,
> And where her present home may be,
> And how she bears life's fag and fret
>   After so long a day?

She is just one fleeting figure, a momentary voice heard in the throng. There are many such, touched unforgettably by Hardy with pathos or humour or an unquenchable vivacity which can turn in an instant to comedy or tragedy. We may bemoan the passing of a favoured custom, the destruction of a notable building, the degradation of a choice landscape; but in the streets of Casterbridge, as in many another part of Wessex, it is the continuity of voice and gesture that links us securely to the midnight scene at the end of the magnificent group of seven poems to which Hardy gave the collective title 'At Casterbridge Fair':

The singers are gone from the Cornmarket-place
    With their broadsheets of rhymes,
The street rings no longer in treble and bass
    With their skits on the times,
And the Cross, lately thronged, is a dim naked space
    That but echoes the stammering chimes.

From Clock-corner steps, as each quarter ding-dongs,
    Away the folk roam
By the 'Hart' and Grey's Bridge into byways and 'drongs',
    Or across the ridged loam;
The younger ones shrilling the lately heard songs,
    The old saying, 'Would we were home.'

The shy-seeming maiden so mute in the fair
    Now rattles and talks,
And that one who looked the most swaggering there
    Grows sad as she walks,
And she who seemed eaten by cankering care
    In statuesque sturdiness stalks.

And midnight clears High Street of all but the ghosts
    Of its buried burghees,
From the latest far back to those old Roman hosts
    Whose remains one yet sees,
Who loved, laughed, and fought, hailed their friends, drank
        their toasts
At their meeting-times here, just as these!

CHAPTER ELEVEN

Conclusion

In my local phone directory there are eighty-eight entries beginning with the word 'Wessex' – from Wessex Academy of English to Wessex World Travel Ltd. I am obliged to make extravagant payments to the Wessex Water Authority, about which I can make futile complaints to the Member of the European Parliament who represents the Wessex constituency. In the naming of parts of England Hardy certainly did not labour in vain. The passing years increasingly consolidate what began as a novelist's device to give a unity to his stories.

Success brings its own penalties and Hardy must often have been troubled, as well as flattered, by the zeal with which his admirers strove to identify in detail each and every mention he had made of village, house, field, pond, cross-road, church, barn or other recognisable feature in the scenes he described. There is no doubt that his chosen method was to put himself in the actual environment that he had selected as his model, and therefore to draw directly from life. Equally he reserved for himself the right to modify, to transpose and to invent. Consequently his attitude to this aspect of his work is ambiguous. He can be willing to offer a conducted tour of the 'real' places to an intimate friend, as he did in the case of *Jude the Obscure* to Florence Henniker, writing to her subsequently, 'What a pity that you never visited any of them with me after all': while at another time he could write to a correspondent, 'You will be surprised and shocked at my saying that I myself do not know where "Little Hintock" is!'

In 1912 the preparation of the Wessex edition of all his prose and verse was the occasion for a considered statement about the Wessex scene as he had presented it. In the general preface to the edition he wrote:

It is advisable also to state here, in response to inquiries from readers interested in landscape, prehistoric antiquities, and especially old English architecture, that the description of these backgrounds has been done from the real – that is to say, has something real for its basis, however illusively treated.

He then added a rider, that 'no detail is guaranteed – that the portraiture of fictitiously named towns and villages was only suggested by certain real places, and wantonly wanders from inventorial descriptions of them'. With that reservation he concluded, 'I do not contradict these keen hunters for the real; I am satisfied with their statements as at least an indication of their interest in the scenes'.

In seventy years the interest has not abated, but what for Hardy was 'the real' becomes increasingly hard to discern in detail as each fresh decade superimposes its layer of new reality. Inevitably some buildings are modified or demolished, landmarks disappear, traditional practices are superseded. Added frustrations in the game of 'Hunt the Hintock' do not however invalidate Hardy's Wessex. The documentary element in his descriptions is valuable but it is not the only one and certainly not the most important.

His architectural training gave him an absorbing professional interest in the buildings of Wessex – and the area is rich in the quality and variety of its examples. He also shared to the full the antiquarian interests of his more enlightened contemporaries in both archaeology and folklore. His contribution there to the general record of Wessex history and custom is considerable and enduring: but beyond all that, and far surpassing it, is the less definable factor of poetic insight, of divination, of imaginative penetration to what I am tempted to call – for lack of anything more accurate – the 'genes' of Wessex. At its finest his is a majestic vision, in which space and time are subdued and harmonised in a coherent scene. He captured, as no-one else had done, the essence of the land which he recognised as the exclusive source of his own life and that of his ancestors.

Always present in Hardy is a feeling of rootedness, of the present time opening into a long perspective where history softens and clouds into legend and tradition; and I believe this is characteristic of the pull exerted by the West Country on those who come under its spell. In the Wessex landscape there is first of all a sense of easy intimacy with our distant past, in the firm and factual terms of Stonehenge, Badbury Rings, the Giant of Cerne, Corfe Castle, Glastonbury – sights familiar to every tourist. And then in addition – as it were, in the interstices of the weave – is the less definable but strongly atmospheric presence of romantic fables and legends, wild and distant imaginings of heroes like Arthur and Tristan.

What Hardy's Wessex embodies so vigorously is this blending of two different levels of experience, two different worlds almost. There can be no doubting the down-to-earth quality of the hard, practical considerations which move his peasant characters. The strain of heavy physical labour was a prime concern of men like Hezekiah Biles in *Two on a Tower*:

> Often have I thought, when hay-pitching, and the small of my back seeming no stouter than a harnet's, 'The devil send that I had but the making of labouring men for a twelvemonth!' I'd gie every man jack two good backbones, even if the alteration was as wrong as forgery.

By contrast with that humorously disillusioned realism there is also an insistent strain of poetry, colouring even the very words Hezekiah uses – a ballad quality that seems to come from some distant quarter to touch the commonplace scenes of everyday life with its strangely imaginative light.

It is this subtle blending – so distinctively his own – which gives to 'Wessex' its permanent and enduring qualities. The forces of change must not be underrated or denied, but we can share with Hardy many of the key-components of his landscape. Salisbury Cathedral, Beeny Cliff, Maiden Castle, the Chesil Beach – these and many another constitute our heritage. They are still the keys to those more profound landscapes of the human spirit that beckoned to Hardy when he contemplated the changing mood of Egdon Heath in the storm of a winter's night:

> Then Egdon was aroused to reciprocity; for the storm was its lover, and the wind its friend. Then it became the home of strange phantoms; and it was found to be the hitherto unrecognized original of those wild regions of obscurity which are vaguely felt to be compassing us about in midnight dreams of flight and

disaster, and are never thought of after the dream till revived by scenes like this.

In such passages as that he achieved his aim that 'that which is apparently local should be really universal'. But it is not the note on which to end. In his Wessex it is more often the case that the universal poetry is incarnate within a plain and local matter-of-factness – as he expressed it in a casual encounter on one of his favourite 'Wessex Heights' in the poem 'Life and Death at Sunrise', which he subtitled 'near Dogbury Gate, 1867':

> The hills uncap their tops
> Of woodland, pasture, copse,
> And look on the layers of mist
> At their foot that still persist:
> They are like awakened sleepers on one elbow lifted,
> Who gaze around to learn if things during night have shifted.
>
> A waggon creaks up from the fog
> With a laboured leisurely jog;
> Then a horseman from off the hill-tip
> Comes clapping down into the dip;
> While woodlarks, finches, sparrows, try to entune at one time.
> And cocks and hens and cows and bulls take up the chime.
>
> With a shouldered basket and flagon
> A man meets the one with the waggon,
> And both the men halt of long use.
> 'Well,' the waggoner says, 'what's the news?'
> '–'Tis a boy this time. You've just met the doctor trotting back.
> She's doing very well. And we think we shall call him "Jack".
>
> 'And what have you got covered there?'
> He nods to the waggon and mare.
> 'Oh, a coffin for old John Thinn:
> We are just going to put him in.'
> '–So he's gone at last. He always had a good constitution.'
> '–He was ninety-odd. He could call up the French Revolution.'

As Hardy himself remarked, 'There was quite enough human nature in Wessex for one man's literary purpose'.

197

Select Bibliography

The New Wessex Edition of Hardy's Novels, ed. P. N. Furbank (Macmillan London Ltd, 1974–6)

The New Wessex Edition of the Poems of Thomas Hardy, ed. James Gibson (Macmillan London Ltd, 1974–6)

The New Wessex Edition of the Stories of Thomas Hardy, ed. F. B. Pinion (Macmillan London Ltd, 1974–6)

The New Wessex Edition of *The Dynasts*, Thomas Hardy, ed. Harold Orel (Macmillan London Ltd, 1980)

The Life of Thomas Hardy, Florence Emily Hardy (Macmillan and Co Ltd, 1962)

The Collected Letters of Thomas Hardy, ed. R. L. Purdy and Michael Millgate (Oxford University Press, 1978)

A Hardy Companion, F. B. Pinion (revised ed. Macmillan London Ltd, 1974)

The Poetry of Thomas Hardy, J. O. Bailey (University of North Carolina Press, 1972)

Some Recollections by Emma Hardy, ed. by Evelyn Hardy and Robert Gittings (Oxford University Press, 1961)

Young Thomas Hardy, Robert Gittings (Heinemann Educational Books, 1975)

The Older Hardy, Robert Gittings (Heinemann Educational Books, 1978)

Thomas Hardy: his career as a novelist, Michael Millgate (Bodley Head, 1971)

Thomas Hardy: a biography, Michael Millgate (Oxford University Press, 1982)

Hardy, novelist and poet, Desmond Hawkins (David & Charles, 1976)

Concerning Agnes, Desmond Hawkins (Alan Sutton, 1982)

Hardy's Wessex Re-appraised, Denys Kay-Robinson (David & Charles, 1972)

Thomas Hardy's Wessex, Hermann Lea (Macmillan and Co Ltd, 1913)

Highways and Byways in Dorset, Frederick Treves (Wildwood House, 1981)

Inside Dorset, Monica Hutchings (The Abbey Press, Sherborne, 1965)

Cranborne Chase, Desmond Hawkins (Gollancz, 1980)

Avalon and Sedgemoor, Desmond Hawkins (revised ed. Alan Sutton, 1982)

Hodge and his Masters, Richard Jefferies (Smith and Elder, 1880, in 2 vols)

A Shepherd's Life, W. H. Hudson (Methuen, 1910)

Early Tours in Devon and Cornwall, ed. by R. Pearse Chope (J. G. Commin, Exeter, 1918)

The Wessex Heathland, Ralph Wightman (Robert Hale, 1953)

The New Forest, John R. Wise (Sotheran, 1863)

The Tour Leaflets of the Thomas Hardy Society

Index